Praise for
AWAKE MIND, OPEN HEART

·■·

"These teachings on how to live with dignity, kindness, and a sense of celebration may be the antidote we need to the depression and aggressiveness of this age."

—MELVIN McLEOD, editor-in-chief of the *Shambhala Sun*

"Cynthia Kneen's *Awake Mind, Open Heart* reveals a well articulated understanding of the newly emerging Shambhala teachings as taught by the late Trungpa Rinpoche. Kneen's book clarifies this tradition, which is at once fresh and ancient, modern and traditional, articulating a practical process of moving from confusion and toward an awake and courageous way of being in the world."

—TSULTRIM ALLIONE, author of *Women of Wisdom*
and founder of Tara Mandala

"An inspiring synthesis of teaching and practice. Kneen's use of situations in which we may apply the teachings make the practice real; yet it is her compassion, her gentle humor and acknowledgment of the human condition that shine through. This is a wise and eloquent work. Since reading *Awake Mind, Open Heart,* my practice has clearly deepened. What more can one ask?"

—DOUGLAS COOPER, M.D. author of *Doctors are Dangerous*

"Cynthia Kneen has written an important book about living our daily lives with courage, compassion, and dignity. Filled with personal anecdotes from her own life and imbued with uncommon openness and clarity, *Awake Mind, Open Heart* invites us to view our world with fresh eyes. Kneen writes with great heart and passion."

—JOHN S. BENNETT, executive director of the
Garrison Institute and former mayor of Aspen, Colorado

"Drawing from her personal experience, Kneen clearly shows how practicing mindful awareness can bring clarity, joy, and peace to everyday experience. These lessons are not designed for ascetic living in remote mountain caves, but rather they are for those of us who have to face the daily challenges of living in the modern world. Under Kneen's tutelage, every event in life becomes an opportunity to discover one's genuine, human dignity. Kneen's clear explanation of these ancient principles help the reader to confidently face the challenges of their personal, business, and spiritual lives."

—LLOYD SARGEANT, executive vice president of
Full Spectrum Lending, Countrywide, Inc.

"Cynthia Kneen presents a heartfelt expression of walking the path of practice. As dharma is planted in the West, newer students can be encouraged by such examples of taking the ancient wisdom traditions to heart. Transformation is not only possible, but much needed in this world. Cynthia has provided a gateway to this journey."

—Venerable KHANDRO RINPOCHE

"Cynthia Kneen's book is an extraordinarily clear, artful, and elegant presentation of the Shambhala teachings. In prose that is at once plainspoken and profound, she opens our sight, touches our hearts, and shows the way to a genuinely transformed life. For an understanding of Shambhala, there is no better or more accessible place to begin than here."

—REGINALD A. RAY, professor at Naropa University,
teacher in Residence at the Shambhala Mountain Center,
and author of *Indestructible Truth* and *Secret of the Vajra World*

"Cynthia Kneen is a feminine warrior, a meditation teacher, a Westerner who has opened for me new vistas of the East. Cynthia reminds me of a verse by Mary Oliver, because she 'is as common as a field daisy, and as singular.' And by reading her book I've discovered that so am I."

—FRED KOFMAN, CEO of Leading Learning Communities
and author of *Conscious Business*

CYNTHIA KNEEN is a senior student of Chögyam Trungpa. She has taught meditation programs for more than twenty years. She is also a practicing management consultant and lives in Boulder, Colorado. *Awake Mind, Open Heart* is her first book.

Also by Cynthia Kneen

AUDIOTAPES
Shambhala Warrior Training

C Y N T H I A   K N E E N

Foreword by David Schneider

AWAKE MIND, OPEN HEART

The Power of Courage and Dignity
in Everyday Life

·■·

A Personal Journey through the
Teachings of Buddhism and Shambhala

MARLOWE & COMPANY
NEW YORK

Published by
Marlowe & Company
An Imprint of Avalon Publishing Group Incorporated
161 William Street, 16th Floor
New York, NY 10038

Library of Congress Cataloging-in-Publication Data

Kneen, Cynthia.
Awake mind, open heart : the power of courage and dignity
in everyday life / by Cynthia Kneen.
p. cm.
ISBN 1-56924-551-7
1. Spiritual life. 2. Shambhala. I. Title.
BL624 K5929 2001
294.3'444—dc21
2001030027

9 8 7 6 5 4 3 2 1

DESIGNED BY PAULINE NEUWIRTH, NEUWIRTH & ASSOCIATES

Printed in the United States of America
Distributed by Publishers Group West

To my teacher, Chögyam Trungpa Rinpoche,
and my mother, Dora Fry Kneen

·■· ·■· ·■·

CONTENTS

FOREWORD

by David Schneider

CYNTHIA KNEEN has always been a teacher for me. I met her first in the late 1980s, shortly after I had begun to practice Buddhism under the social vision of Shambhala. By that time, I had done sixteen years of Zen and had had the good fortune of meeting great masters from many traditions. I knew what it felt like to be around sincere practitioners and skillful teachers. Cynthia's composure, elegance, and worldliness impressed me immediately; but there was something more. One had the feeling that here was someone who had done real work, here was someone who had looked straight at herself, worked on what she saw, and accepted herself in an uncompromising way. I think you will feel this directly as you read through these stories.

Awake Mind, Open Heart is full of teachings about the path of meditation and bravery, and yet somehow I can't see it only as a book of teachings. Much more to the point, it's a book of translation. I feel this perhaps because I've lived in Europe the past eight years, and concerned myself with translation of Shambhala Buddhism into the cultures here. My teacher, Sakyong Mipham Rinpoche, remarked recently that if the teachings were to really take root in Europe, they would need to be given, discussed, and tested in the mother tongues and in the native cultures. (He'd noticed that in Germany, his German attendants had politely spoken English with him, but when they wanted something done with urgency, they'd spoken German with one another; the same in France with French attendants; the same in Holland with Dutch attendants, and so forth.)

Ms. Kneen, of course, speaks and writes in a very clear American English. It is also indisputable that both holders of the Shambhala lineage—Vidyadhara Chögyam Trungpa Rinpoche and Sakyong Mipham Rinpoche—have given teachings in a remarkably penetrating English. So by "translation," I do not mean from a foreign tongue into American English. I mean rather translation from whichever place and time and culture the wisdom originated, into our culture, here, today. We the readers are the ultimate, intimate destination. We the readers should be personally affected.

To put it another way, an "ordinary" American woman—nobody special—studied with highly realized Asian meditation masters. This woman tried out the teachings personally, followed them to the depths of their profundity, and has now been generous enough to speak about them in everyday terms. To speak so—in everyday terms—is regarded as the most difficult way to teach.

I suppose I should also admit that "translation" is equally an inadequate word for this process. What has really been accomplished is transmission: the delivery of wisdom from India, Tibet, Japan, China, Shambhala, North America, South America, or wherever, to your doorstep, into your hands.

The most common image for such transmission—a meditation tradition coming from one culture to another—is that it is like holding a flower next to a rock and hoping that the flower will grow. This image is mostly brought out to console us (we're the rock end of the deal here, in case it wasn't clear) and to say that yes, surely it will take a while, one mustn't get depressed or discouraged. But Cynthia Kneen's book is also evidence that something can be done. She, for example, has shown with her life, and now with her words, how to crumble a little, how to soften and aereate and let things in; how, in the end, to crack open the rock. The tradition has taken grateful root in her. Here is a blossom from her flower.

A word of warning: It won't do any good to rush through this book, only to have read it. It's not about knowing what's written here, it's about trying to live what's written here. This is rich material, and haste is antithetical to it. Please take it slowly, and enjoy.

TENSHO DAVID SCHNEIDER began Zen practice in 1970 and was ordained as a Zen priest in 1977. He is the author of *Street Zen* and the coeditor, with Kazuaki Tanahashi, of *Essential Zen*. He lives in Cologne, Germany, where he serves as director of Shambhala Europe and as an *acharya* (senior teacher) of the Shambhala International community.

AWAKE MIND,
OPEN HEART

INTRODUCTION

▪▪ ▪▪ ▪▪

Ground: The teachings of Buddhism and Shambhala
are very profound.

Path: When we take them to heart.

Fruition: We can gain courage and dignity,
regardless of our circumstances.

MY first introduction to Buddhism was when I visited Tassajara, a Zen Buddhist retreat center in Big Sur, California. I had
been hiking in the High Sierra with friends, and we heard that
this particular retreat center on the coast had wonderful sulfur
baths. A bath is paradise for a hiker, so we decided to drive there
to visit. It was the end of a hot summer, and the air was already
clear, crisp, and sparkling with the coming fall. I was also curious about Zen Buddhism. As I was bathing in one of Tassajara's
private pools, an autumn leaf floated gracefully by and fell next

to an exquisitely placed vase, which had a single flower in it. I remember thinking that very moment, "If this is Zen, it isn't for me. This experience is too clear, too expressive, too heartbreakingly beautiful, too pure. I'm too emotional and wild for this." After bathing, we waited to meet the Zen Buddhist master, Shunryu Suzuki Roshi, but he was ill and couldn't see us that day. Instead he sent us a message saying, "You are welcome to come back, or you can come to Zen Center in San Francisco." Then almost as an afterthought the message continued, "Also, there's a Tibetan teacher in Colorado who's very good."

Before leaving Tassajara, we participated in a meditation session to see what it was like. The meditation hall was dark, the cushions that we sat on were black, and the robes on the resident practitioners were black, too. One person walked around during meditation with a big stick and hit several people on the shoulders, which made me curious and tense. Then the residents chanted something in Japanese, and finally the meditation session was over. I went outside, and a sheet of paper tacked to a bulletin board was flapping gently in the breeze. It caught my eye, and so I read it. It was an English translation of what I had just heard chanted in Japanese—the *Heart Sutra*, an extraordinary Buddhist text on the nature of reality. To me it didn't describe reality as something remote, scientific, or mystical, but as the sense perceptions and thoughts I was experiencing that very moment. Reading this text changed my life.

When I returned to the East Coast, I wrote to Tassajara for a copy of the text and asked how I could begin to study Buddhism. A resident sent me the *Heart Sutra*. However, she also said that Roshi was now dying of cancer, so I went on about my life. I began to practice hatha yoga to relax my mind and help my body be more flexible. One day my hatha yoga teacher said, "You *must* meet my teacher, the *high* Tibetan lama, who's traveling on the

East Coast." The emphasis on high was so strong that I thought, "Good grief, now what?" But the *high* Tibetan lama turned out to be Suzuki Roshi's "Tibetan teacher from Colorado," Chögyam Trungpa.

In my first private interview with Chögyam Trungpa, he asked if I knew how to meditate. I said, "Not really. I sit, but I don't know what I'm doing." He said, "Show me what you do." So I rested my mind in a simple, nothing special way, and he said, "That's it!" Then he leaned forward and said, "Now, *do* it." "Now, *do* it," I have discovered over the years, is the harder part. Rinpoche (*Rinpoche*, like *roshi* or *sensei*, is an honorific title for an accomplished teacher.) immediately sent me into a three-day solitary retreat where I was miserable—restless, buried under an avalanche of thoughts, and so on. That marked the beginning of a new phase of my life. I began to study and practice Buddhism in earnest. Chögyam Trungpa became my root teacher. In Buddhism a *root teacher* is a teacher from an unbroken lineage of practical experience that has been handed down since the time of the Buddha, who in turn shares this practical experience with you personally.

What I present in *Awake Mind, Open Heart* is based on my study and practice of Buddhism and, later, of the social vision of Shambhala as taught by Chögyam Trungpa and his son and current lineage holder, Sakyong Mipham. Studying *kyudo* (Zen archery) with Kanjuro Shibata XX, Imperial Bowmaker to the Court of Japan and a Japanese National Living Treasure, furthered my understanding, as has the companionship of many friends, experiments I've done in business, Shambhala Training workshops I have taught for many years, and the simple unfolding of my life. It is my hope to share some of my understanding of Trungpa Rinpoche's original teachings on Buddhism and especially Shambhala in a way that allows you, the reader, to make your own personal connection to their meaning.

The teachings of the Buddha are profound and vast. They have been studied and practiced widely throughout Asia since the Buddha taught in India twenty-five hundred years ago. In contrast, Shambhala, a asocial vision based on individual bravery and a conviction about the beginning less goodness of human beings, has been taught widely only recently, so Buddhism is old and venerable, while Shambhala seems very new. Yet Shambhala is believed to have thrived as a tradition of enlightened social relationships and enlightened bravery in Central Asia prior to the Buddha's time. Many scholars believe the Buddha taught his highest teachings in an Asian kingdom called Shambhala, lying to the north of India. As Buddhism spread from India to flourish in Tibet from the ninth century until the recent Chinese invasion, the teachings on a Shambhala social vision were kept alive within the Buddhist monastic community, although they were taught only to an elite few. In 1959 Trungpa Rinpoche, an important young Buddhist abbot, escaped from the Chinese invasion by leading a party of followers over the Himalayas to take refuge in India. This remarkable story is told in his book, *Born in Tibet*. The party left hurriedly one night, and Chögyam Trungpa left behind many personal and monastic belongings, including several important Shambhala texts. Trungpa Rinpoche subsequently studied in England and taught Buddhism in Scotland and North America. I met him soon after he arrived in the United States, and I began to study the Buddhist tradition under his guidance in the 1970s. Then, although he was already regarded as an extraordinary translator and transmitter of the complete teachings of Buddhism to the West, Trungpa Rinpoche began to translate and teach specifically Shambhala meditation texts with what seemed like sudden force, so I began to study this tradition, too. Finally when Chögyam Trungpa died in 1986, Dilgo Khyentse Rinpoche, one of the most respected Tibetan

Buddhist teachers of the twentieth century, said in a private interview that the entire purpose of Trungpa Rinpoche's life was to bring the Shambhala teachings out, these very ancient social teachings that had been kept alive within Tibetan Buddhism and only transmitted to a select few. If this was the entire purpose of his life, then it is important to transmit this knowledge so that it can thrive in the world.

On the whole, the relationship with a teacher is not easy. Over the years, for example, it seemed to me that when Rinpoche told others to be meek, he told me to roar like a lion. When he told others, "Jump the gun! Trust yourself, you've come a long way, you won't kill your friend," he told me, "*Don't* jump the gun!" This was confusing. Always profoundly compassionate, once he growled into my face for a moment that seemed to last forever, "Get mad, get mad, get really mad! Get angry!! Grrrrrrrrrrrrr!! Grrrrrrrrrrrr!!" Another time I said something, and with a wild Tibetan grin no more than two inches away, he clenched his teeth, growled, and shook his jaw, "It's good, it's good, it's really good! Push! Get angry! Grrrrrrrrrrrrrrr!!" This is pretty typical of personal encounters with a teacher. You study and practice intensely, so that when they personally instruct you, the instruction penetrates straight to your heart, to your hang-ups and your wisdom. Their kindness strikes like lightning to burn what's in the way. At the same time, you have layers, and layers, *and* layers of thickness, so it's difficult to put their instructions into practice. That, of course, is the journey part.

As I think back on my experiences and write this book, currently we are experiencing a severe drought in the western United States. During a drought the land, and all it supports, is very stressed. Horses become lame from standing on earth that's hard as rock. Trees droop and their leaves whither and hang. With a tree, its leaves are sacrificed to maintain life in its core, so the life of the tree isn't anchored in its outer display anymore. It gives it up. Something similar happened to me in the 1990s. I experienced an extended series of shocks, losses, illnesses, and injuries. Having been a more or less enthusiastic student and teacher of Buddhism and Shambhala for many years, I found that I had less and less to say about the teachings and, finally, nothing at all.

As I look back, I think I was like a tree in a drought, sacrificing an outer display in order to save life at the core. In many ways, for me this book is a coming into expression again. In the process I have learned that being on a path of courage and dignity is always messy, just as life is always messy. In the Buddhist and Shambhala traditions you are not trying to achieve introspection or mystical transcendence, but inner authority so you gain full presence in the world. Therefore the journey includes everything you do, can and will experience. It has successes, failures, bruises, joys, deep holes to fall into and climb out of, and vast playgrounds for compassionate expression and activity. It is, as they say, life itself. Being depressed and defeated doesn't mean that you're not on a path. A friend recently said to me, "It's the broken person who has to teach now, not the person who's on top of things. In our world today being broken is a position of power, because you have to navigate according to the heart, rather than according to outer things." Your personal journey and the details of your life are never separate. Just because you are devastated, there's no escaping the need for courage. Just because you are successful, there is no escaping fear. Even though you are afraid, where will you go? What will you do? Where will you run to? Even when you are running away, you are there with yourself. Courage and dignity are always timely.

Although I can pinpoint when I encountered certain teachings, I have been on a journey for as long as I can remember. I believe this is true for each of us, because it is the nature of being human to be on a personal journey. Therefore any teaching you or I take to heart, regardless of where and how we receive it, is not a set of concepts we can just put on and take off like a suit of clothes or a good idea. This is because we can't just put on and take off that longing, intelligence, and sense of meaning we call our purpose, our integrity, our soul, our bone and marrow. There is no real beginning to a personal journey, just as a personal journey has no real end. For me, trying to practice the Buddhist and Shambhala paths has been, and continues to be, precious, lucky, messy, and sometimes downright terrifying. I am extremely grateful and, at the same time, a slow learner. For example, it wasn't until Trungpa Rinpoche was sick and dying that I realized that I simply, uncomplicatedly, loved him, and that his teachings were simply, uncomplicatedly, a gift of love.

I chose to call this book *Awake Mind, Open Heart* for several reasons. What we usually call *mind* is very rich and complex in its expression. It has aspects of consciousness, subconsciousness, thoughts, awareness, perceptions, memories, elations, depressions, and so on. Yet in its essence mind is very simple. In the Shambhala and Buddhist traditions the essence of mind is openness and clarity combined, or openness inseparable from the capacity to know. It is inherently curious and tender or warm. Therefore I use the notion of *awake* mind to suggest that, generally speaking, this mind you or I have doesn't seem to be as open, clear, curious, and sympathetic to the world as it could be. It doesn't seem to be all that awake. Instead, this mind you or I have is often busy, emotional, and discursive, too unpredictable one moment and too predictable the next. Sometimes your mind is wild and other times it is stuck. When you look at it closely, it is crowded by thoughts that often aren't very sensible. Or it is so sluggish that you can't perceive the simplest things happening around you or with yourself. Yet when you look at your mind directly, it doesn't do anything. And in another moment your mind is brilliant, and your senses are vivid and clear. Generally speaking, this mind doesn't do what you want it to do! In contrast, the notion of an *awake mind* is a mind that is open and sympathetic to see clearly what's what. It is a clear mind that simply and fully illuminates what it perceives. In this sense "mind" is like a tool you can use, and you want this tool to do what you want it to do! You want it to be clear, brilliant, sharp, and powerful all the time.

I chose *open heart* to indicate a sense of inherent sympathy to the world, courage and dignity. When we say we did something "with heart" or "wholeheartedly," we mean we engaged ourselves without hesitation and without holding back. We were able to relate fully. So heart is some kind of guts you have in you to open and extend yourself, to feel things fully and properly, to be challenged and to learn. It is your willingness to engage and then actually doing so. Anything you do can be openhearted or halfhearted, like tasting a peach, scratching an itch, or talking to a friend. You are either fully engaged in your experience or not. An open heart means that the essence of yourself is in play, and that is how you attain a sense of dignity. By dignity I mean full or authentic presence in the world based on an inner journey you have made. You are able to take a bigger view of the world around you, because you aren't purely preoccupied with yourself. You are able to be touched by and to touch and influence your world, because you have made a personal journey to open up and engage. Having an open heart goes farther than having an awake mind. It takes more strength and energy because the world's energies are powerful. Therefore courage and dignity are essential in daily life.

I have divided *Awake Mind, Open Heart* into five parts that loosely reflect the stages of a personal journey, from discovering there is something unconditionally good, open, tender, and even valiant about yourself, to developing an awake mind and open heart in the detail and grit of your daily life, and finally, having been of benefit to yourself, to becoming of benefit to others, too.

Part I, "Basic Goodness," discusses our basic resources as human beings. It introduces the notions of warriorship and basic goodness, which are important in both Buddhism and Shambhala. The path of the warrior is based on using awareness of basic goodness creatively and compassionately in everyday life. Part II, "Settling Down with Ourselves," lays the groundwork for how to actualize ourselves as gentle and brave. In my training this requires the experience of meditation, so I have included meditation instruction, as well as how to work skillfully with fear. Part III, "Courage in Everyday Life," focuses on the resources we have to be gentle and fearless in everyday life. As anyone can experience, when you are open, gentle, and fearless, all kinds of chaos, potential chaos, and accomplishments are possible. It's as if you had removed a layer of your own skin, so now you are more sensitive to the world's glamour, its energies, its tricks and power. This section therefore includes instruction in a warriorship practice to rouse your *windhorse energy* or *confidence.* Believed to come from the great clans of ancient Mongolia and China, this practice increases individual spiritedness and strength to connect to vision, so you can engage more powerfully with the unique incidents happening in your life. The result is gaining a presence in the world that is compelling, sympathetic, and dignified. Part IV, "The World as Friend," introduces the notions of sacred world and lineage and examines dignity in depth. Finally, Part V, "It's Our Turn to Help," contains reflections on leadership and change and expresses the conviction that it is, indeed, our turn to help this world, which needs our help. Parts IV and V are like water in a well. Water fulfills many purposes, but water in a well doesn't fulfill any purpose until you put a dipper in it, draw the water out, and put it to use. I discuss the water in the well, but I leave the selection of the dipper to you. I share some of my own experiences in this arena, but I have largely left specific applications to the reader.

You will notice a three-line stanza at the beginning and end of each chapter of this book. Buddhism often employs a three-part structure to develop the logic of a given subject. This logical structure is sometimes called *ground, path,* and *fruition.* For example, (1) water (2) is wet, and (3) irrigates fields and quenches thirst. (1) Buying a ticket, (2) getting on a plane, (3) we arrive at our destination. Or, as in this Introduction, (1) the teachings of Buddhism and Shambhala are very profound, (2) when we take them to heart, (3) we can gain courage and dignity, regardless of our circumstances. The application of *threefold logic* as an analytical tool can be very powerful. Chögyam Trungpa taught his students that if we didn't have a sense of these three things, if one or two of them were missing, or if we couldn't distinguish them, there might be confusion in our experience, our understanding, or both. I have made each chapter's threefold structure explicit, not because the logics are especially elegant, but in order to demonstrate a method that others might find useful. You can use it to help you in conducting your work, talking to your kids, thinking through what's puzzling you, negotiating with your car mechanic, or anything. In particular, threefold logic is a way to look at a total process and therefore to develop knowledge that is inseparable from intuition and real experience.

Over the years, in addition to studying Buddhism and Shambhala, I have been active in the business world, holding various low-level, medium-level, and senior positions with reasonable success and influence. I now consult to businesses on aspects of leadership, data-based decision making, and effectiveness related to innovation and strategic change. Although my meditation practice influences everything I do, professionally I have always kept my interests in Buddhism and Shambhala private. Now, however, it seems like a good time to share these teachings further. If we look around today, this world we have is obviously an awe-inspiring and powerful place. Equally, it seems to be in terrible shape. There is so much each of us can do to help this world.

I wrote this book to illuminate for you a few themes from Buddhism and Shambhala that have been meaningful to me, because I believe these themes hold meaning and hope for our time. I hope you feel encouraged to explore and begin to use meditation and *windhorse* practices in your everyday life. If you can practice meditation so that one or two meaningful thoughts come through from all the myriad thoughts you have, that's good, not bad. If you can do just one action in your whole life that skillfully benefits others, that's also very good.

Awake Mind, Open Heart is neither a philosophical treatise nor a practical manual. It does not replace the original teachings of Chögyam Trungpa, who transmitted these two distinct traditions, Buddhism and Shambhala, and during the time he taught in the West (1970s and 1980s). Instead, it presents personal reflections on aspects of these teachings that have been, and continue to be, meaningful to me as a student and practitioner of these ways. These are Chögyam Trungpa's teachings as he gave them publicly, privately, or in small groups, which I repeat or say in different ways. It is personal in the sense that I use personal stories and experiences to articulate certain themes. In particular, I have tried to present aspects of Buddhism and the social vision of Shambhala that a reader unfamiliar with either tradition might find intriguing and then useful in everyday life.

In many ways the actual message of Buddhism Shambhala and is simple. It's that our everyday world is completely workable.

You may be in a terrible mess, or those around you may be in a mess, but it's a workable mess. This is because there is something unconditionally good, without exception, about all human beings. Dignity, courage, simplicity, compassion—these are your heritage purely by being human. They are your potential. The main theme of courage is being individually brave enough to uncover your own potential, appreciate it, bring it into your everyday life, and use it to be of benefit. I hope this book will give you an authentic, although partial, introduction to Shambhala and Buddhism. But in particular I want to encourage you to make your unique journey today without losing heart. I want you to enjoy and engage this world we have.

Whether you are alone on a desert island, in solitary confinement, sealed up in your car on a freeway, or alone with your thoughts and longings, you still have a world. We are always in the world. It's *how* we are in our world that matters.

On the whole, the purpose of these Buddhist and Shambhala teachings is entirely to bring out your courage and dignity in whatever your circumstances. My hope is that you will feel supported by *Awake Mind, Open Heart* to appreciate your life and to unabashedly, without apology, help make this world a better place to be.

PART ONE

Basic Goodness

·■·

1

The Meaning of Shambhala

·▦· ·▦· ·▦·

Ground: The social vision of Shambhala has many meanings,
and one of them is personal.

Path: By finding its meaning in our experience.

Fruition: We are able to uplift ourselves and our society.

WHEN the Shambhala meditation texts were first introduced
by Trungpa Rinpoche, people said, "This isn't Buddhism. What is
Trungpa doing?" The texts are on warriorship, dignity, sensory
richness, how to rule one's world—not typically Buddhist texts.
Similarly, when Mipham Rinpoche, a great Tibetan Buddhist
teacher of the nineteenth century, talked about confidence practices
and going to the northern country of Shambhala after he died, saying he was needed there, people thought he was becoming senile.
They thought, "This isn't Buddhism. What is Mipham doing?"

At first glance, Shambhala is not fully, solely, or even obviously Buddhist. It doesn't openly rely on the historical Buddha Shakyamuni's teachings. It doesn't emphasize the truths of impermanence and interdependence in the same way that Buddhism does. Instead, it looks directly at the warmth and power in our ordinary sense perceptions. It doesn't teach by logical reasoning that your ideas of good, bad, you, me, tree, ground, sky, bird, desk, car, job, school, country, yesterday, today, and so on are empty of lasting identity. Instead it goes straight to the experience of "basic goodness," an intangible energy that you can experience now, in you, and in your environment, that is constantly present in shifting experiences. Rather than relying on study and scholarship, anyone can see and use these teachings. The Shambhala teachings are earthy and secular in this way. Yet the heart of Buddhism is based on personal experience, the source of the Shambhala teachings is very closely connected to the Buddhist *vajrakilaya,* the Shambhala teachings on basic goodness are very close to the notion of Buddha-nature, and the experience of sacred world in Shambhala is very close to Buddhist teachings on pure perception. There is an impression among Western audiences that Buddhism is rather bleak, while Shambhala isn't. Yet when the Buddha attained enlightenment, he didn't say, "Woe is me." He said, "Wonder of wonders." The entire Buddhist path is based on the discovery of egolessness and the maturing of insight that comes from this. It reaches from discovering "four noble truths" (suffering, how our suffering comes about, the true nature of things, and how to conduct ourselves to lead to an end of suffering) to celebrating energies and life. Although Shambhala doesn't use the language of egolessness very much, the central experience of basic goodness is the experience of open space, nonego, the principle that things are empty of duality. The gaining of a warrior's genuine dignity is the maturing of this insight. And both of these great traditions look closely at our individual experience, without shying away from what's negative, and draw conclusions that are hopeful, compassionate, and highly practical for creating a decent life and a good society.

Ultimately, and for practitioners who are like myself, the traditions of Shambhala and Buddhism are not far apart. They are like two eyes that together function to create excellent vision. Each is about creating a shift in how we see things and, in that way, going beyond caring for ourselves alone. In Shambhala this is called the path of warriorship and in Buddhism the path of compassionate heroism. The result of both traditions is increased power in our ability to effect events around us, and the attainment of boundless compassion, compelling presence, and enlightened enjoyment of our world. In neither case is the creative energy of the tradition about personal growth alone. Both have an extraordinary positive social vision.

The Shambhala lineage was introduced by my teacher, Chögyam Trungpa. But Shambhala, like Buddhism, was not just made up today. There have been many methods throughout history and in different cultures to try to help us cultivate who and what we are as individual and social human beings. These are ancient teachings about having a brave, strong, and noble heart. Shambhala comes from a warrior tradition of Asia that predates the spread of Buddhism from India, but Shambhala belongs not only to Asia. It resonates with the teachings of other cultures throughout the world and throughout human history. There have been, and are, pockets of Shambhala all over the globe—in South America, North America, Latin America, the native Americas, Persia, Africa, Europe, Korea, Japan, New Zealand, and other places. The meaning of Shambhala has been with us, within us, constantly for a long time. Shambhala uses the mindfulness-awareness doctrine developed by the Buddhist tradition, which is discussed in Part II, yet mindfulness-awareness is as old as human life. The Shambhala teachings on the confidence-rousing practice called *windhorse,* which are presented in Part III, have their roots in ancient China and Mongolia, but every culture tries to capture and harness the exuberance and energy of life.

Shambhala is a lineage of teaching for humans, from humans, on how to manifest dignity and human power in everyday life, and how to use our brain, eyes, ears, emotions, and everything we have to realize the all-pervasiveness of basic goodness. Meditation, unconditioned confidence, natural wealth, *windhorse* energy—these things are inherent in human beings. They are part of us. We have had them for a long time. Because of tendencies in ourselves and society, we forget, so that being fully who and what we are as a human being becomes something to accomplish.

Our challenge is to take our human inheritance personally. Particularly in today's sectarian and divisive time, we need something that can accommodate all genuine traditions trying to develop human beings, so that together we can build a society based on gentleness, fearlessness, and a reasonable way of life. Fundamentally, Shambhala is a nonsectarian view that looks directly at our experience to find the principles of how to organize society. This is not easy, but it has been done; and therefore we can do it, too. This requires that we make ourselves at home in the unconditioned, enjoy our life, and never, ever, give up on ourselves or anyone else.

In Buddhism there are often said to be *outer, inner,* and *secret* meanings to a teaching. We can say that *outer* is the literal or external meaning; *inner* is the psychological meaning, the meaning you and I hold in common just by being human beings; and *secret* is self-secret, the intimate meaning you find in your unique experience, and I in mine. The secret meaning isn't good or bad.

It is simply, fully, what it is, as it is, on the level of personal experience. We can apply these notions of outer, inner, and secret meanings to the Shambhala teachings themselves. In fact, these notions are like three aspects or stages of finding any teaching meaningful. The teaching isn't really changing. The meaning is becoming subtler, and *you* are changing. Each stage penetrates more to your heart, bones, and marrow. What you understand is becoming more personal.

For example, the *outer* or *external* meaning of Shambhala is the notion of an actual good or enlightened human society, here on this earth, whether existing in the future, the past, or the present. In this meaning Shambhala is a secular society that actually exists, where people live long, peaceful, and productive lives, where society in all its relationships is organized on the basis of conviction in universal goodness and human dignity. Some scholars believe a kingdom called Shambhala existed in Central Asia during the Buddha's life-time, probably in Mongolia or present-day Pakistan or Afghanistan. Trungpa Rinpoche is said to have been expert at being able to look into a mirror or the palm of his hand, see the literal kingdom of Shambhala, and describe it in great detail. Yet sometimes he would say about this ability, "People are just being polite." Actual texts and maps still exist about how to find Shambhala, and even when people say the Buddha taught there, it's understood that the goodness of this society transcended a religious outlook alone. This outer meaning of Shambhala has inspired travelers, explorers, anthropologists, and historians for centuries. It inspires movies like *Lost Horizon,* and it is probably the basis of our Western notion of an Eastern paradise or Shangri-la.

The *inner* meaning of Shambhala is that a vision of an enlightened society is natural to human psychology. A vision or archetype of a good society exists in you and me whether such a society existed, or ever will exist, historically or not. You can find this vision in philosophy, leadership studies, teachings, children's stories, rituals, and in all cultures' myths and legends. Throughout history governments come and go, but people have had a notion of Shambhala that has lasted throughout the best and worst of human history. Anne Frank's diary expresses this conviction in human goodness. A musical composition, a mathematical equation, a flash of kindness from someone on the street, can express conviction in human goodness and a good society.

I used to have what I called refrigerator art, where I put newspaper articles and photos that inspired me on my refrigerator door with magnets: a lady who lived alone in a tiny rental apartment and left a fortune when she died to do good works to help society; a photo of a woman surgeon who operated on gang members in the emergency room after they shot each other, and then taught them how to work with conflict in her extra time; a prescription I received from my internist when I had a lot of grief and he wrote on his prescription pad, "Eight hugs a day." Photos, art, articles—anything that inspired me went up on the refrigerator door. I thought, "I can take heart from others who have courage and a vision to help." In Tibet there are paintings that depict various kings of Shambhala. Nicholas Roerich, the twentieth-century artist and explorer, invoked the idea of Shambhala when he enlisted nations to protect cultural monuments during the First World War. People throughout history have had a vision or longing for a good human society on this earth, as people do today. This longing for a meaningful life is natural. You and I use it like the North Star to move toward, or sometimes to move away from, what we consider to be good and excellent. All humans have an intrinsic vision of positive human potential.

The *secret* or *self-secret* meaning of Shambhala is somewhat different. Here each of us has to engage the essence of our individual existence to find its meaning and relate with its reality. In this meaning Shambhala already exists now in your own experience. It is completely accessible and available—it's simply up to your individual bravery to find it and display it more. This self-secret meaning of Shambhala exists in your opening to the vastness of a single sense perception, in an instinct you have toward courage and dignity, or simply in your longing to communicate. I believe the greatest concern of Trungpa Rinpoche was to teach and share this self-secret meaning because this is the one that strikes to our heart and our difficulties today.

It may seem outrageous to proclaim it because often you don't feel this way, but the self-secret meaning of Shambhala is an innocent, wholesome, powerful, and not naive conviction you can have in the goodness of life. Shambhala in this sense is a pattern of energies that are rich with vision, pragmatic, realistic, and enjoyable that lie just below the surface of everyday consciousness. These energies can be mined like a treasure, as if there were something in your own experience temporarily hidden from your view that could help you. In this analogy you are the treasure hunter and also the dig site. You are the one who has to dig beneath the surface and do the manual work to bring Shambhala out, because its enlightened energies can be completely hidden from your view. Some event may have to happen to shock you into looking more closely at your experience in order to find it. This event might be a car accident, the birth of a child, a dream, an unexpected disappointment, an unexpected success, or an encounter with someone who seems to experience a goodness or sacredness to life that you don't see. Up to that moment you may not be looking for anything meaningful in your life, or you're looking too hard, or you may not be looking in the right place, or you're not using the right method. Maybe you don't care to look, or your purpose isn't clear, or it's too difficult to look, or you're preoccupied with something else. Then something causes you to shift and look more closely than usual, and a little deeper, at your own experience. And this shift makes all the difference.

The secret or self-secret meaning is that Shambhala is a subtle aspect in your everyday experience and you only have to shift your attitude slightly to discover it. The analogy of Shambhala as a hidden treasure is that its value is intrinsic and accessible, but you can't see it. Something is in the way, and whatever that is—misunderstanding, unfamiliarity, laziness, discouraging yourself—needs to be removed. Like gold, jewels, or oil that are hidden in the earth and completely close at hand, the value is there. But when you don't notice it, it's as if it doesn't exist. You look around and don't see anything inspiring, so it's as if the treasure isn't there. You think, "Ho hum, there's nothing happening here in my experience." Then when you discover the treasure, you say, "Oh. It was there all along. It was covered up. I didn't see it before. I didn't see what was in front of me!" When you see it, nothing has changed, except *you* opened up. Your perspective shifted. Now you see what was hidden from your view. Once you see it, you have conviction about its value. "I thought the meaning wasn't important." "Now I see its value." Once you discover the meaning of Shambhala in you, you know how to use it and you know what to do.

There was a famous gardener who taught at the University of California in Santa Cruz named Alan Chadwick. He gardened by growing soil to grow plants, and what he meant by soil was different than the earth's surface that you or I usually mean. I think he may have meant a power in the universe that could be concentrated in gardening to capture cosmic magic. Chadwick grew soil and planted seeds based on relationships that exist between the earth, its moon, the sun, the other planets, the weather, the way doves in the area coo, mist in the trees, and everything you could imagine. When winter was very bleak, he'd sing about the

Alan Chadwick Gardens
: basic goodness & ordinary magic

energies underneath the surface of the earth. "Underneath the seeds are full of life. Life! This very moment the seeds are waking up! They're pushing up to the sun! The doves are singing, 'Coo, coo.' Life! Life!" Once Chadwick took a class to a junkyard lot that was filled with rusted-out cars, broken glass, chunks of cement, sand, and lots of abandoned trash. He asked the owner if his class could use one section of the lot for an experiment to grow flowers and vegetables. The owner said, "Sure, but you're crazy. That soil's dead." This garden later became famous for its extraordinarily delicious vegetables and gorgeous flowers.

The secret meaning of Shambhala is similar to this. It's like an open secret. You are the inspired gardener, the junk, the earth, the seeds, and the junkyard owner, too. To the inspired gardener in you there is a natural wealth and wisdom in your everyday experience that you usually ignore. It only needs to be uncovered and displayed. This takes energy, exertion, and courage, but it benefits you and everyone. To the junkyard owner in you, this doesn't seem practical, but the gardener in you is intrigued, so the junkyard owner goes along. You're willing to investigate and see what you learn.

Once I lived in a fledgling Buddhist meditation center in the northern part of Vermont. I held various jobs—head cook, practice coordinator, work coordinator, financial auditor, and so on. It was tough—mostly male practitioners and a few women living in an old farmhouse with drafty windows. We lived on a modest budget, with winters that reached thirty and forty degrees below zero and gardens in the summer where we picked worms off the cabbages by hand. We barely kept our cars and relationships going.

Everything we did was threaded together with regular study and meditation. We were studying Buddhism with Trungpa Rinpoche, who used to meet with us individually and give house talks and public seminars. The Shambhala texts and social vision had not been introduced yet. Once at a house gathering Rinpoche gave a slide show of photographs he had taken. A small group of us was sitting in the farmhouse living room, and he showed a close-up shot of a beautiful flowering shrub with spectacular pink blossoms. It was breathtaking. I said, "Oh, how beautiful!" It seemed so far away to me. "Where did you take that?" It was a photo of a bush in the meditation center's front yard. I wasn't looking in a way that I could see what was right in front of me.

Years later I was part of a senior management team in a large corporation, and I had the same experience. I realized that our team was literally blind to internal barriers to the company's success. Others on the team realized this, too. We weren't looking in a way that could reveal the interactions that were happening in the company or with ourselves. Too many habitual pressures and habitual assumptions were in the way. We thought, finally, that if we want to transform the organization, we're going to have to change ourselves.

Finding the secret meaning of Shambhala in your own experience is a process of personal discovery that takes energy and exertion. Like finding gold, jewels, or oil in the earth, you have to work to find the meaning and make it yours. What does Shambhala mean to *me*? What can I *do* with it? As you make it your own, your understanding becomes more effortless because, in the process of making it your own, you engage your heart. Engaging the heart takes courage. Therefore Shambhala is sometimes known as a *warrior tradition* because it is based on the notion of being a brave person. The warrior brings her mind, body, and heart together at a single point in a single moment to open to the world. This takes practice and experience, and it also takes courage.

As a warrior, you can be a government worker, an ambulance driver, a mother giving birth, or a person on one side of a conflict.

What makes a Shambhala warrior is not that you fight with bombs and guns. You might also be a soldier, but that's not what's brave about you. Your bravery is that you engage the essence of your individual humanity as you do what you do—while you drive a cab, write a memo, give birth to a child, and engage in a conflict. Your bravery is personal. You trust in your humanity and in your own kind of intelligence. You have gained sympathy or compassion for experience, your own and that of others. This is an indication of your courage to be a human being. And so you become known as a particular kind of warrior, a person with a positive social vision, a person with a noble heart.

Your bravery isn't so much about changing what you do. It's about changing *how* you do what you do, and this has an effect on your environment and yourself. You still eat, sleep, make love, talk with your kids, handle your dilemmas, drive a car, walk down the road, take a bath, do your laundry, look at a sunset, listen to the news, engage in a conflict, and water your plants. The difference is that, as a warrior, you have developed a noble heart to appreciate life. You try to create, protect, and promote the energy of life in everything you do. And you have gone beyond caring purely for yourself and your world to caring for others' well-being, too. This is not easy, yet in both Shambhala and Buddhism the warmth to care for others is seen as natural to human beings.

There is a subtlety in your everyday reality that you usually don't proclaim, yet the self-secret meaning of Shambhala is that this subtlety is the foundation for brave and compassionate relationships. To explore it, you need to look at what is *primordial* or *essential* about yourself, what is original or not created in you—that natural essence that is intrinsic, ordinary, and always there. When something is natural, it isn't made up and it doesn't go away. It is at the level of things as they are. You can't even say it is basic or nonbasic—it just is. In order to find bravery and a positive social vision at the heart of ourselves, we need a method to help us look at and uncover the essence of ourselves, and we need encouragement. The great humanistic traditions give us these. In Shambhala and in Buddhism the method is largely phenomenological. It starts with what's closest to you, which is your own experience. You look at yourself without judgment to find out what is essential about human beings. You investigate your everyday reality directly, without the usual labels of good and bad, right and wrong. *Directly* here means immediately, or looking into this present moment, now, with as little interpretation as possible.

Lovely description

As you sit at your desk, as you listen to traffic passing by, is there something in your nature now that has intrinsic value as a foundation for integrity, decent relationships, a good domestic life, good organizations, good institutions, and a good society? If you can find something of unconditional value in your personal existence as it is, then with a little effort and courage you can create a shift to bring it forward and stabilize it, so it is with you all the time. You can use it to uplift yourself and your surroundings, and in this way benefit yourself and everyone else.

To begin to access the secret meaning of Shambhala, ask: Is there something in my existence now, as it is, that has value intrinsically, on its own, that I'm not seeing? Something naturally there that is not dependent on how I was brought up, my I.Q. or personality, my race, gender, nationality, or ethnic group? Something that has innate value personally and as a foundation for good relationships and a good society?

2

Basic Goodness

·■· ·■· ·■·

Ground: There is something unconditionally
good about ourselves.

Path: Experiencing our soft spot, we glimpse a larger world.

Fruition: We can use these glimpses to discover a path of courage.

THE very first principle of the Shambhala teachings, the ground of individual bravery and social vision, is realizing that there is something unconditionally good about yourself. *Unconditionally good* means a goodness that is natural or not created, not man-made. It doesn't depend on conditions or circumstances such as your education, your money, or your luck. It exists before all the conditions you experience in your life. *Unconditioned* means it is always there: it isn't manufactured and it won't go away.

As you look at your experience now in this moment, as you dig a little bit below the surface of your everyday concerns, you can discover you have a huge softness that pervades your sense of being. There is something in you that can be touched by what you experience, no matter what it is. Maybe you hear a dog barking, a cricket chirping, cars on the road, wind moving through the trees, a television in another room, voices, a refrigerator humming. You feel the fabric of your shirt on your skin, your eyeglasses on the bridge of your nose. You hear someone call your name. Just simple experience. Underneath the experience there is an enormous softness or openness, which is intangible and pervasive, that allows you to experience these things. In Shambhala this is your basic being or nature. It is primordial or fundamental and always there. It is simple, clear, and open like the sky. And like the sky, this openness is extraordinarily ordinary, powerful, and unfailing. Its sensitivity enables you to accept and incorporate energy in an uncontrived way, no matter what you experience. Intrinsic openness is there whether you are in your car, in your kitchen, walking in a field, sleeping, arguing with your partner, or riding on a bus. It doesn't matter whether you are male, female, Australian, African, tall, short, young, old, fat, thin, a criminal, or a saint. It doesn't have anything to do with your beliefs or your religion. It is more fundamental than that. It is a basic nature, an openness without bias, a capacity you have to have your own personal experience.

The notion of being intrinsically without bias is important. As you dig just below the surface of your beliefs and expectations, you can see that situations are very fleeting, that some kind of energy is always happening in life and you don't control it. The world just presents itself in the moment without filter, and you open and incorporate its energies without a filter, and that's how you experience. That's how you learn. This absence of filter is openness without bias. Something is happening, and you have a tenderness, a sensitivity to incorporate what is happening now that is powerful and unbiased like a mirror. This complete acceptance exists at the prethought level of your experience. It is miles down the road before you judge things as pleasant or unpleasant, right or wrong, good or bad. The world presents whatever it presents in the moment, and this basic sensitivity in you reflects whatever is happening and accommodates it spontaneously without editing it, like a mirror.

Trungpa Rinpoche called this openness a *soft spot,* because it's like a spot you have that's so raw and tender that when you touch it, you feel something. In the Shambhala tradition this is your humanity. Your soft spot allows you to experience the warmth of the sun, a little bug's journey across a windowpane, an ache in your shoulder, or anything. Without it, you wouldn't be human or alive. Without this fundamental softness or openness, you couldn't experience a tree or a cloud, hear the sound of a garbage truck in the morning, laugh, sneeze, or shed a tear. You wouldn't be human. You'd be a brick. But instead you are a human being.

If you were asked, "What is the human thing in you?" you would probably feel uncomfortable. You might say, "It's the same that's in you. Why are you asking this anyway?" Still, as we look directly, we can see that this vast soft and sensitive spot is what makes us human. You may take it for granted. You may have to work hard to drop your concepts of good and bad to find it, but it's there every moment in a raw and uncomplicated way. It's at your service. The world presents itself, and underneath your thoughts and actions you accept what the world presents. Underneath your conscious activity you accommodate and reflect what the world presents and reflect it without a filter. This is how you have a direct connection to reality.

This intrinsic openness has different names in different cultures. There is a Peruvian story from the High Andes about a young warrior who always wore a mask, even while he was sleeping. A young Q'ero village woman was enchanted with him. One night as the warrior lay sleeping, she crept up and opened the visor of his mask to see his face. Behind the mask there was nothing but a vast and brilliant blue sky. In the symbolism of this story your essential nature is like a vast and brilliant blue sky. Like the young warrior in Peruvian legend behind his mask, there is a clarity and openness that you *are*. Buddhists call this open state "buddha nature." A Zen master calls it "big mind." Quakers call it "God within you." The Q'ero village Indians might say that the sky and stars in the night sky only appear to be outside; they are really in *you*. What these traditions are referring to is a monumental capacity each of us has to be touched, to have personal experience, to have experience at all. Although it has different names in different traditions, it's there for anyone to see. It is our open secret as human beings.

This soft spot is the source of our humanity and the source of our creativity. It allows us to function and live our life. It is because of a complete mirrorlike acceptance in us that we can appreciate or reject sounds and colors, want to be a soldier or an artist, make a pizza pie or soup, have opinions about the weather, skin our knee, have an inner life, or try to mold the world around us. Fundamental openness is operating all the time in our everyday life, however much we take it for granted. "Umm, good scotch, burnt hamburger, blue tie, sunny day" are possible because of this mirrorlike acceptance in us. We *have* freedom to interpret and create experience because we *are* freedom, just like the Peruvian warrior can *be* a warrior, because he *is* open sky. We *are* openness, therefore we can *be* open in everyday life.

In Shambhala this basic capacity is called *basic goodness*. It is what's good about you—unconditionally good, because it is good without being compared to bad. It is good because it is natural. It is *so*. There is an accepting energy in you that doesn't have any struggle or aggression in it. It is unbiased or mirrorlike, and it is good because it functions to give you unique and personal experience, whatever your experience may be.

It's difficult to accept a notion of goodness that isn't good compared to bad. I used to wish basic goodness were called something else. But what should we call it? *Basic goodness* is called *basic* because it's always there, like earth, sky, and the elements are always there. And it is good because it functions well. There is a workability in our experience, a fundamental trustworthiness that's just there that allows us to experience our world. That aspect of trustworthiness or workability is goodness. Trungpa Rinpoche said, "We don't really, at the bottom of our hearts, complain that there are a sun and moon, day and night, trees, the colors red and yellow, or the wind. These are natural. They are so much a part of our everyday life that they transcend complaint." Maybe *this red* is too loud, or *these trees* block the view from our window. But in our heart of hearts we trust the redness of red and the presence and power of trees. We don't really resent the functioning of natural things. The logic is that basic goodness is the absence of bad, because there is nothing *wrong* with it. It accommodates. It provides service. It is good.

When basic goodness is in you, Shambhala calls it your soft spot. But on an ultimate level, basic goodness is the principle of nonduality or open space that is always in the background, whether it manifests or not. Rinpoche called it diamond-like or indestructible, because basic goodness in itself doesn't have any bias toward good or bad and therefore you can't destroy it. It is unfailing. You can't wound it or slash it. You can't destroy it. It isn't changed by your realization of it or lack of realization of it. Basic goodness is in you and in the cosmos. It's not particularly mystical. If you want to grasp it, it is simple and open. It is intangible, but it is there. If you look for a cause or a beginning of basic goodness, you can't find one because it doesn't have ordinary boundaries. You can't measure it because it's not external in that way. It transcends ordinary proof. You can ignore basic goodness, but it never goes away. It is huge and vast, yet when you reach to grab hold of it, basic goodness is nothing at all. If you want to *say* it, you end up making grunting sounds like, "Sky, house, tree, you, me, blue, red, emotion, thought, existence—it works." Our existence is good because it *is*, because it is *so*.

We can discover basic goodness in a simple experience of *nowness*. I used to live in a cottage in sunny California. The house had French doors, pegged hardwood floors, a vaulted ceiling, and lots of open windows with gardens outside, so lots of spiders lived there with me, too. I had long hair, and I was also very busy at the time, so I didn't dust much. Some of these little spiders had very long legs. Often a stray hair of mine would get caught in a crack in the wood that had fuzz and dust collected in it. And a spider would get one of its long legs tangled in it. When this happened, that spider had to work to untangle itself from its predicament of a leg caught in hair and dust, and the long-legged ones worked especially delicately. Sometimes as I would watch one of these little spiders work to free its leg from hair and dust, the experience of nowness would hit me. When I would watch the long-legged spiders work, I could feel that something real was taking place, that the spider had its predicament, I had mine, too, and we were connected in a way that had its own uniqueness and power. This experience is ordinary. It has no duality or sense of time in it. Instead there's a sense of pervasive goodness that exists on its own authority, purely inspired by sense perceptions, without self-consciousness or hopes and fears, in this case, without hopes and fears about the spider, myself, or life and death, its own or mine.

Usually we ignore experiences of basic goodness because we don't know how to integrate them or what their purpose is. These experiences are complete on their own, just simple and direct, without duality in them. They are the ultimate nonaggression. Falling snow presents its uniqueness and power to you without saying "Shovel me." A spider disentangling its legs from dust and a strand of hair displays its elegance without saying "Help me" or "Take a photograph of me." A smile flashes without saying "Get to know me, like me." What you perceive makes a total statement, and the statement wakes you up to the goodness and beauty in things. It wakes you up to a connection between your wisdom and the wisdom in the world around you. When you experience things fully, without struggle, your experience has the quality of joy and well-being. It is complete. It doesn't refer to anything else. It is enjoyable. You feel naturally elegant, just as the snow, spider, and a sudden smile are naturally elegant. You appreciate being a human being with sense organs, living in a world of five elements, with a mind that reacts and is able to perceive and appreciate.

It's embarrassing to discuss basic goodness. This goodness is too simple, too obvious, too excellent, too close to home. What's the point of mentioning it? It's so basic—no wonder we forget about it. And, what good does goodness *do*? Besides, it may make us feel a little lonely to acknowledge basic goodness. The experience is too personal, too puzzling and provocative, too naked. It isn't a religious or mystical experience. It isn't aesthetic or philosophical. It isn't even logical or illogical. It is something you experience that isn't tied to any one particular circumstance. You can't predict when it will occur. Nor is the simple, unpredictable experience of goodness caused by anything in particular. You can't plan to have an experience of basic goodness, although you can organize your life in such a way that you have more awareness of it when it does occur.

Ultimately basic goodness is the principle of nonduality. Perceptually you experience it as no separation between yourself and what you perceive. It manifests as a sense of trustworthiness and workability in your experience where you feel you are able to connect with the wisdom in phenomena around you. These real experiences of goodness do occur. You can have a real experience of basic goodness as you are stepping out from a refreshing shower, feeling the weight of a utensil in your hand, or watching a child sleep. When your mind is relaxed and going along naively with things, a sudden openness and clarity can hit you. You experience a gap in your thought processes. Your mind is neutral, innocent, and without agenda, and for a moment you have a precise and vivid awareness of basic goodness. These experiences are unpredictable and unplanned—and they do occur. Maybe you are smoothing the morning sheets, and out of the blue you become aware of the textures and colors of things—the colors in the fabric, the wrinkles in the sheets, a breath of fresh air you take in, the morning sunlight, the feel of cloth on your palms, a moment's peace. In that moment you glimpse a larger world that isn't sorted into workable and not workable, pure and dirty, good and bad anymore. Your energy is accepting and appreciative, without struggle or aggression in it, so your insight and your sense perceptions are experienced as one superbly good working base.

In yourself this good and trustworthy working base manifests as a gentle, sensitive, tender, huge, and powerful soft spot that you experience when your perceptions don't have any struggle in them. This powerful soft spot allows you to be touched by a tie you'd like to wear, a threatening look, the suffering of someone on the news, a smile, or smoothing out your morning sheets. And it also manifests as a spark of interest, as your appetite for experience. Your own curiosity, inquisitiveness, intelligence, and willingness to be challenged—these are indications of basic goodness in you, too.

My first solo retreat I was afraid. I didn't know how I was going to handle the dark. The cabin was very small and isolated, and I had a very strong thought that murderers would come through the woods, chop me into bits, and put the parts in a locker in a bus station in some obscure town. No one would ever find me again. So every night I put an ax that I used for splitting wood and a flashlight next to me. I trained myself to sleep with my hand on the ax. My retreat went along without adventure for a while, and then one night it happened. A murderer came for me. I could hear him in the cabin in the dark. It seemed like it took forever for my hand to reach the flashlight. Then I switched on the flashlight and raised the ax to strike. The murderer was a tiny, furry brown field mouse. If you've ever seen a field mouse, they are really very, very small. Its heart was pounding so hard in its chest that its whole body was booming. We hung there together in the moment for a long time, both our hearts pounding, and then the moment passed.

That little field mouse taught me a lot. Each of us was believing in a fantasy. The mouse wasn't thinking what I was thinking, and I wasn't thinking what the mouse was thinking. It didn't see pajamas, a sleeping bag, pots and pans, and I didn't see the richness a little mouse could smell, or eat, or store. Yet our paths had crossed. Both of us were inquisitive, both of us were willing to take a risk, and both of us were afraid. What was really real? For a while I thought the real situation was peaceful northern Vermont, summertime, a human being, a wooden shack, a surrounding field with tiny mice. Then I thought that reality really was that both the mouse and I were brave. But now I think that reality was the basic goodness that accommodated and supported the fields, the woods, the retreat center, bus stations, murderers, the sun, the moon, courage, fright, the field mouse's fantasy, and my fantasy. The little field mouse and I each had a soft spot, and we were each fabricating a fantasy, but we didn't know it was a fantasy. What was real was basic goodness, which showed itself when our paths crossed.

That little mouse helped me contact basic goodness. On a Shambhala warrior's path, our only reference point is basic goodness and that's what we learn to project confidently in everything we do. But neither the little mouse nor I had the wherewithal to project basic goodness with confidence. Yet maybe we did contact it naturally, tentatively. I was aware the little field mouse had a soft spot and I did, too, and we weren't really different. It wasn't that my soft spot was the bigger one, and the mouse's soft spot in its tiny body was littler. A soft spot isn't measurable in that way, because basic goodness isn't a little bit vast over here and a lot vast somewhere else. I could see that the tiny mouse's curiosity in the moment was just as huge and boundless as mine, and its tenderness was huge and boundless, too. Basic goodness was in me, in the little mouse, and equally in the flashlight, the ax, the pots and pans, the field, the scraps of food, the hills of northern Vermont, the bus station down the road, and nearby Canada.

Reference points are all the details that occur in our lives. Anything you do is made up of reference points. As you drink tea, grind your teeth, shed tears, rake the lawn, admire a friend, turn on your television, paint your lips with lipstick, drive your car, and brush your hair, there are billions of details happening. When you have basic goodness as your only reference point, it doesn't mean you aren't functioning. It's more that nothing is in the way of your functioning properly. You are able to relax your mind, so your whole being is open, flowing, and not fixed on anything. A student once asked Trungpa Rinpoche, "But how can you *function* like that?" He said, "Oh, you function much better! A person who's aware of basic goodness can walk down the street, chew gum, and catch the right bus much better than you can!" A person, or a little field mouse, who's aware of basic goodness is not caught or fixed on any fabrication but is open and appreciative while doing what they do.

When basic goodness is covered up, you feel claustrophobic or uninspired, psychologically and spiritually backed into a corner, subtly suffering, trapped. Yet when you acknowledge that you do experience basic goodness, even when your outer circumstances haven't changed, you find yourself able to accept, appreciate, and work with what the world presents. Nothing is startling or threatening, because when you are aware of basic goodness, whatever is happening isn't separate from yourself. The moment has a flowing and also a superbly stable and steady quality. You feel connected. Your body and mind are synchronized. You feel you have possibilities in your experience, that you are never, ever really trapped. Yet basic goodness hasn't changed—you have.

The entire path of courage is learning to adopt basic goodness as your reference point, so you can live without being trapped in fixed concepts, without having hidden corners psychologically and spiritually that make you struggle to perceive. Just your mind is open and strong because you've settled into basic goodness in you, in others, in your phenomena, and in the cosmos. Then you can deal with relative situations with ease and elegance.

Basic goodness is the unobstructed energy in everything. It is in us and between us. It allows you to function and communicate. From it you can create hostility or humor, love or war. It is your individual capacity to cry, to be fearless, to see the blueness of blue, to experience the four seasons, to feel love or anger, or anything. This ability or power in you to have genuine, real experiences is very potent and monumental, and it resides in your heart, whether that heart is cowardly or brave. In Shambhala this gentle soft spot, this basic goodness, is what we have in common with each other.

There is basic goodness, the experience of basic goodness, awareness of the experience of basic goodness, and using awareness of the experience of basic goodness as you do what you do. Ultimately, on a path of courage you are trying to increase the latter one. This takes energy and confidence. But just by accumulating glimpses, you can begin to care for others' humanity too. Once you can do this, you are ready to begin to tread on a warrior's path.

3

Being Genuine and True

·■· ·■· ·■·

Ground: Being friendly to ourselves.
Path: We are genuine and true.
Fruition: And therefore we project harmony to our world.

THE first step in gaining of courage is to recognize that you have a soft spot and that you experience basic goodness. There is basic goodness in your experience, whatever it is. The next step is to soften to yourself, and be genuine and true. Not *true* in the sense of true versus false, but true in the sense of real. You're trying to stay in contact with the reality that's taking place with you, first of all. To do this the very first thing to do is to bring out the texture and flow of your own energy. If you are depressed, afraid, elated, or bored, what is the experience? What are its qualities?

What intelligence is in it? Your interest in yourself is simple, gentle, and direct. This kind of paying attention to and appreciating the textures of your own energy is being friendly to yourself or having sympathy for your own experience. This is an intelligent thing to do. It is the essential first step of courage, whatever your experience is.

The basis of friendship, with yourself or anyone, is not to get something done. You don't make your friends justify their appearance in your life. Instead when you see them coming, you soften and open up. "Hey! What's up? How are you doing? What's happening with you?" You love them and are sympathetic, whatever they are going through. So regardless of what you are experiencing, first be friendly to you. Provide a big space for yourself. Open up, accept and respect yourself. If you are bored, let yourself be bored. What does the boredom feel like? If you are panicked, be genuinely and truly panicked. What is it like to be panicked in this way? If you are grieving, expand your grief instead of trying to cheer up. See where the grief wants to take you. Even if you are afraid, don't try to make your experience different. Don't try to fix it, ignore it, or even understand it. It's too soon to fix it, ignore it, or understand it. Just be genuine first of all. Just bring out the texture and flow of the experience you are having, whether it is boredom, panic, loss of strength in your heart, or anything.

There is basic goodness in joy, in depression, in rage, in sneezing. There is basic goodness in success and failure. A soft spot is always there underneath the surface, so first of all don't hassle yourself. If you are having an experience of sadness or anger, let it be that way. Do you feel joyful? Depressed? Fine. You don't understand something? That's good—that means you *could* understand. Are you dying? Are you living? Bring awareness to what you are experiencing without judging yourself. This is the kindest and most realistic thing you could do—to accept and respect the experience you are actually having. You are taking the first action of a Shambhala warrior by staying in contact with you.

This is not easy. It is difficult to provide a big space for ourselves. Right at that moment something tends to go wrong with our mind. We harden up. "It's too risky to soften up." "I don't have time." "What's the point, anyway?" "It makes me feel hopeless and lonely." "It will destroy me." "Feel my painful experiences? This is asking too much."

Right here there is something we have to learn. It's as if our mind has never really had a friend. It's not very trusting, so of course it doesn't do what we want it to do. It's restless, nervous, and doesn't trust very much. When we open and relax to our experience, as soon as things get vivid, our mind tends to jump. This doesn't have to be dramatic as in an experience of pain or grief. Simply look at the blue of the sky. As the blue starts to penetrate, your mind looks for something more—a plane, a cloud, the sun, a horizon, anything. It's as if your mind were saying, "Yeah, yeah, blue sky, so what? Come on, move it along." Generally speaking your mind wants some other occupant than the one it has. It looks for a substitute to what's happening. This may be particularly true with painful experiences, but even with pleasurable experiences the mind is restless.

Generally, you experience what you experience, then you have ideas about that, and these two aren't synchronized. Your experience and your ideas about your experience aren't in harmony. When you look at the blue sky, your experience of blue and your ideas of the plane, the clouds, the sun, and yourself don't really mesh. You shift away from your experience a little bit, and that shift rapidly begins to magnify. Now what you project to others isn't harmonious either, because you have become confused about what you're experiencing and what you're trying to achieve.

Your ideas are going one way, and your experience is going another. You want to react to what *the others* think about blue sky, the sun, and airplanes today, even if the others you are projecting are imaginary and fabricated, just made up in your mind. If you get a hint of your confusion as you relax to experiencing the blue sky, instead of being *genuinely* confused, you block your thoughts and jump to something else. You feel you should be having an experience different than what you're having and be someone other than yourself.

Not only is the mind generally pretty restless and unused to having a friend. The way we approach things tends to harden our heart. We judge who we are, what we are, how we are, where we are, why we are, and what we are experiencing, so it's difficult to have compassion for ourselves. There is a courtroom in session going on in our mind. When the judge comes in, we stand up at attention. "What am I doing, Your Honor? Good question! Yessir! I should get back to work, or I should have more fun! Whatever you say!" We have a tendency to reduce ourselves to one intense little dot of earnestness and purpose. "I've got to do something about my relationship with my spouse." "This dirt on the floor, this food in the refrigerator—it has to go." We do this with anything. "I need to toughen up." "I need to soften up." "I need to look at the blue sky." "I need to look away." The judging mind tends to shrink its target unnecessarily. It separates us from our experience.

All this adds up to a lot of confusion and disconnection. When we are at work, we want to be on vacation. When we are on vacation, we want to be at work. We jump from one thought to another very fast, until we lose a sense of what we are trying to communicate or what we're trying to fulfill. We don't feel the situation. There are gaps where we don't know what is happening, and instead of experiencing the gaps we produce more thoughts, more interpretation, more misunderstanding. This is what we project, and the world reflects it back.

You are arguing with someone. In a moment of openness you relax to the other person's pink cheeks, his youth, his mustache. He has a sense of humor. He's funny! And instead of letting the humor penetrate, instead of letting the communication evolve in its own way, your mind jumps to get back on track. "Wait a minute—where's my anger? Whose side am I on anyway?" Having lost track of yourself, you lose track of the other, too. "What's he thinking? Where's he heading? What does this mean?" So the first act of individual bravery is to soften and be yourself. You are trying to find your own wisdom, and it starts with you.

When you are able to be genuine in this way, something happens. It makes you feel gentle and awake. As a young girl learning how to wear high heels, I learned to walk in high heels in the living room. Then I learned to walk downstairs to the living room from upstairs. Then I learned to walk downstairs, my knees parallel and to the side, so I looked feminine. Then I practiced walking downstairs, knees together, feminine, keeping my inner power strong, thinking, "Don't show how hard this is." Then I practiced walking downstairs, knees to the side, feminine, inner power strong, relaxed, imagining a boy in my eighth-grade class at the bottom of the steps. "Hello." Then I practiced . . . and on it went. I felt tender and brave, genuine, a young girl trying to be gentle and awake, soft and tough, simultaneously.

In Shambhala gentle and awake together, soft and tough together, is the ideal state of being genuine. In fact, softness *is* the toughness. Be *genuine!* This softens your relationship to everything, including yourself. Gentleness *is* the strength. Human beings *should* feel soft and good. Instead of looking for another experience or judging what you are going through, the first advice to awaken the courage is to be yourself at all costs. I have a friend who tells me, "Be yourself at all costs." Everything splendid about a human being—dignity, courage, gentleness, integrity, humor, sharpness—begins with being genuine.

The analogy Trungpa Rinpoche used for being genuine was holding a brick of solid gold in your hands. Not fourteen-carat gold, but a brick of one hundred percent pure gold. If you were holding a brick of solid gold, the experience of it would feel full, rich, real, and true. "This is solid gold. It's the real thing." In the same way, when you are genuine, there's a sense of being without obstacle. You feel fundamentally healthy, unified, full of substance, full of something real taking place. "Here I am, sad." "I feel crummy." "I feel great." "I love you. It's true-blue." "I'm confused. It's the real thing." Because of being real and true, you also feel resourceful, wholesome, and aware that you are leading your life in the fullest way. You can't be talked out of your genuineness. If others around you seem to be fake and not true, that's simply things as they are. So be it. You are true as you are, and that's reality, too.

There is a story of the Buddha's enlightenment. After years of effort and austerities to try to understand who he was, what his experience was, and how his mind and body worked, finally this young Indian prince decided to change his whole approach. Nothing was working, so he decided to sit down and be as he was, without struggling, and not get up until he realized something. This young prince then ate the first nutritious food he had eaten in a long time, and he sat down in a simple posture beneath a bodhi tree in northern India. During the night his realization began to unfold, and the young prince became the Buddha, the world enlightened one. As his realization began to occur, the Buddha was attacked by doubts—demons and hallucinations, fierce projections, fierce thought processes. Instead of trying to block the experience, the Buddha continued to let go of struggling to change himself. Finally at dawn a fierce projection of the cultural norms of India at that time rushed at the Buddha and demanded, "Who are you to resist me? Who says you are enlightened? Who says you are awake?" And the Buddha—*buddha* means "awake" in Sanskrit—didn't say anything. Instead, he touched his hand to the earth in a gesture of complete sanity and ultimate genuineness.

This gesture said, "The earth is my witness. My experience is real. It transcends thought processes and ordinary proof. This experience is one hundred percent genuine and true. It is unfolding without stopping." Therefore the Buddha is known as a completely accomplished, fully human person—a genuine, true, and therefore superhuman being.

The experience of genuineness occurs whenever you are harmonized, whenever your body and mind are harmonized through relaxing and being kind to yourself. When you are in touch with yourself, when your experience and your ideas about your experience are the same, then what you experience and project are wholesomeness, healthiness, unity—a sense of trueness. You are at home with yourself. You present yourself as one unit, together, without complication. Your energy radiates out; it's natural, continuous, and flowing. "It was great. I relaxed and was myself." In a moment of laughter, when you are genuine and you laugh, your body laughs and your mind laughs, so everything is synchronized. There is a sense of flow, warmth, invincibility, and trueness. You are unconditionally being yourself.

Now your energy can naturally evolve into something else.

When you are genuine and true, whether in a job interview, making love, talking with your colleagues about politics, gardening by yourself, or negotiating with a client, your body and mind are in the same place. There is a sense that the world is a friend, that you can take the next step. "I stopped struggling, and then things worked fine." You have real possibilities. This is the enjoyment aspect of basic goodness. Maybe the activity you are engaged in is very mundane. You are about to cough, that's all. Or you are communicating something endearing to your child or your pet. The scale of your activity doesn't matter. Whether you are talking over the fence to your neighbor or talking to your colleagues at the UN, when you are genuine there is a sense that the relationship is open and it will work. The social communication will be true. You can extend as you are. And because you experience harmony in yourself, you project that to others, too. You project healthy energy, and it communicates capability, warmth, and wholesomeness to your world. Whatever our circumstances, this is how we begin to create a good and wholesome society.

When I was growing up, I had a friendship ring. It had little chips of stone in it, and one tiny chip was missing. I wore this ring for years. When I looked at it, sometimes the flaw would be showing and sometimes it wouldn't. Whether the chip would show or not was unpredictable and always caught me by surprise. Each time I looked it reminded me of something but I didn't know what, so every time I saw the flaw or no-flaw, I came back to just being myself. This is a game a teenager plays, as she's trying to grow up. I felt it was important to come back to myself, although I didn't know what I was coming back *to*. When you come back to being genuine, it's like this. You can remind yourself to be yourself over and over, moment to moment. It is a simpleminded practice, and very powerful.

In order to create a decent society, first of all we need to treat our own experience with decency. This is the hardest thing for all of us to do , and it's the hardest thing to do moment to moment. But a good society has to begin as simply as this. When you apply friendliness, sympathy, and compassion to yourself, you project harmony. If decency doesn't apply to you, you can't apply it anywhere.

4

A Joyful and Sad Heart

·■· ·■· ·■·

Ground: Experiencing our experience fully.

Path: Our heart is joyful and sad.

Fruition: We develop conviction that a joyful-sad
heart is natural and good.

WHEN you experience unconditional goodness, you may not
know what to do with it, but the experience touches and awakens
your heart a little bit. This is joyful, simply because it is enjoyable
to feel warmth in the area of your heart. You might associate this
kind of joy with activities like gardening, listening to rain falling
on a roof, or being with someone you love, but this kind of joy in
your heart isn't tied to any particular cause or circumstance. It
arises whenever you relax and are gentle and sympathetic to our

own experience. Your energy is released and flowing. It is unob-structed, and this warms your heart.

When we say a person has *heart,* it doesn't mean they are weak and sentimental. We mean they are willing to be exposed, willing to be touched nakedly by the world. They are strong enough not to wear a suit of armor. They are not afraid of their experience. In this sense heart is the one hundred percentness of experience. It is a strength and fullness in you that come from putting your awareness in the actual experience you are experiencing. This is true even of negative experiences. With a strong heart you are able to be gentle and sympathetic to all your experiences, not only the pleasant ones.

This is not easy. Usually we resent negative experience as an intrusion into our psychological space. In dark times we think, "Life isn't meant to be this devastating or bleak." Or if we have a "total experience" of anger, we don't really mean we had a heart-felt experience of anger. We mean, "I was so mad I had to use everything in my power to sidestep what was happening with me." Now I am in conflict with my experience, and one of us is going to win, my experience or me. But a heartfelt experience of anger, grief, sadness, joy, fear, boredom, or desire doesn't have this kind of resentment or struggle in it. When you are gentle and sympa-thetic to your experience, you're not trying either to suppress it or to get rid of it by acting it out. Instead, when you put your aware-ness in your experience, there's nothing extra for you to hang on to. You are just left with the fullness of what's happening. You are left with the energy. You have a direct and full experience of what's happening, instead of trying to manage the different elements of a conflict—you, the object of your emotion, and the emotion itself.

It may not feel like it at the time, but the more awareness you bring your experience, the more it strengthens your heart and your intelligence. This is the joyful aspect of being a human being. Plac-ing heartfelt awareness in your experience deepens your understanding of how things are, whether it is experience of the fragrance of a flower, your fondness for a favorite pair of earrings, anger at another driver, desire for a particular kind of ice cream, grief, or anything. The strength and fullness in your heart at that moment produce warmth, which naturally expands. The joyful aspect is that you want to spill your heart. You would like to share your genuineness. You would like to go beyond your limits. You would like to communicate your experience fully, whatever it is. This is a natural process, a natural longing in you. As a human being, you long to share the fullness of your experience—and then you discover that you can't. This is a central insight in Shambhala's social vision. You can never, ever, fully communicate your experience to someone else. This isn't a *flaw* of being human. It's *being* human, and the unrequited longing your experience produces a subtle joy that is slightly sad. It produces joy because when experience is heartfelt, you are not fabricating, editing, or manipulating anything. You are genuinely being yourself. Your experience of genuineness has longing in it to communicate because you feel there is something positive in you, and because it's very positive it is joyful and tender. Yet when you try to share your experience fully, you find you can't. You are trying to share your soft spot fully with someone else, but your soft spot is monumental, huge, and vast. In the process of trying to capture it, it becomes something else. You can never fully capture and communicate your soft spot, and so your joy at being genuine is always a little sad.

This experience of having a joyful and sad heart is called discovering *the genuine heart of sadness* in Shambhala. And being able constantly to be in touch with a joyful-sad heart is how you evolve into being a decent human being. You have to be a little sad to feel your soft spot; therefore the person with a noble heart, the warrior in touch with his or her humanity, the person with an unfailing conviction in human goodness, is always joyful-sad.

During a program on breast cancer on National Public Radio a young single mother of two girls was interviewed. She had had a lumpectomy and radiation treatments a few years earlier, and now a recent blood test had found that the cancer had spread to her bones, liver, skull, and other places. She was worried about her girls. "Did the older one know how to operate the dryer? Who would help the littler girl learn how to ride her bike?" She said, "I was very depressed. I felt such a heavy burden." Her neighbors decided to get together and pray for her. On a Monday night they came over and prayed, and whenever anyone wanted to say something, they would. "I told the group that what I want more than anything is to change my attitude. I can't live with this darkness and feeling a heavy burden like this." That was her prayer.

Tuesday morning when she woke up, as she described it in the interview, "The sun was streaming in my window. It was pouring in, and it seemed so beautiful. I sat up and looked across the street at my neighbors' house, and their daffodils were golden. They weren't just bright yellow. They were radiant. They were glowing. I couldn't wait to tell my family what had happened to me." She added, "Now I know I'll be all right. Even if I'm not going to be all right, I'm going to be all right, if that makes any sense." About five months later, she died. I think she died with a brave and joyful-sad heart.

Being gentle and realistic, like this young mother, is the unique experience of joy and sadness joined. Connecting to joy and sadness together paradoxically means you are able to smile. Out of the experience of basic goodness, out of joy and sadness joined, comes a pragmatic tenderness to appreciate and be sympathetic to your situation, to see the basic goodness of *this* particular world you have, *this* difficulty, *this* aloneness you experience, *this* brilliant color yellow, *this* child in front of you, *this* joy, *this* pain, *this* love, *this* fear of dying, *this* fear of living, *this* experience.

According to Shambhala's social vision you should *always* be joyful-sad because it puts you in touch with basic goodness; without being in touch with basic goodness, you wouldn't stay genuine and true. For the fledgling warrior sadness is essential because it makes you more susceptible to feeling things fully. It helps you be compassionate and stay in contact with the true energies that are happening in a situation and with yourself. It keeps you sympathetic to the colors of the world, the energies around you, and the experiences of someone else. Without sadness you lose a genuine sense of nowness. You begin to fabricate another now than the one you have, and you and I slip into a subtle phoniness, where we are blocked from being present and our experience seems corrupted or slightly fake. So having a genuine heart of sadness indicates you haven't corrupted your humanity by trying to be someone else, be somewhere else, or be present without longing in your heart.

Once Kanjuro Shibata XX, Sensei, the Imperial Bowmaker to the Court of Japan, and one of my teachers, said in broken English at the end of a *kyudo* (Japanese archery) class, "Hello means good-bye. My hope, hello again." I thought, he's right. Hello *does* mean good-bye. Everything is impermanent; nothing lasts. We should really say "Good-bye" when we shake hands "Hello." But then Sensei also said, "My hope," which is also true. I think he was communicating the genuine heart of sadness. When you are brave and have an open heart, you have affection for *this* world—*this* sunlight, *this* other human being, *this* experience. You experience it nakedly, and when it touches your heart, you realize this world is very fleeting. So it is perfect to say "Hello means good-bye." And also, "My hope, hello again." Just experiencing experience openly makes you joyful-sad.

Somehow, when you stay open and are able to feel your heart without shutting down while you smell a lilac in the garden, hear rain on the roof, see the yellowness of daffodils, watch your daughter ride a bike, or contemplate dying, it adds up to joy and sadness. And experiencing these two together, joy and sadness, builds up your goodness and decency.

Now genuine communication with others becomes possible because by opening your heart you extend to others and simultaneously are human to yourself. A traditional Buddhist analogy for having a fully human heart is radiation without a radiator, like warmth radiating without a source. This kind of radiating is an endless supply of warmth that we have purely from being a human being. It is activated by being genuine. It doesn't need any other spark or fuel. You simply have to be yourself to release natural warmth, so there is less you have to do, not more. Simply open your heart, first of all. When your heart is open, the warmth that is released puts you more in touch with the world's real energies, and this affects your heart more, which releases more warmth, which allows the world to touch you more, which further activates your heart. It's a little like nuclear fission. You have an endless self-renewing resource of unconditional warmth in you purely from being yourself. This isn't warmth to fix, conquer, or do anything in particular, so when it is released, it's unguided and undirected. It goes everywhere.

In the Buddhist and Shambhala teachings the more you release this heartfelt energy, the more it warms your world. The more you open to yourself, the more you see what you have in common with others. This puts you in genuine communication with other human beings, and out of warmth comes skillful activity. You see that you're not alone, that you share this world with others who are just like yourself, who have the same hopes, sorrows, and longings. They care for their young, defend their homes, reach out to help another, and want to live a decent life just like you do. Now you know what others feel. This is joyful. At the same time, the more you see what you have in common with others, the more you realize each person without exception, is also individual and unique, each one is always ultimately alone, and each one of us loses touch with basic goodness. And this is sad.

Joy and sadness together are essential for genuine social bonds. Left to its own rhythms the warmth in our heart evolves naturally to skillful communication. Yet the warmth in our heart isn't left to its own rhythms. And although a joyful and sad heart is natural, to use an open heart as the basis for communication and society takes patience, practice, and bravery. It is difficult to go beyond our limits, to go beyond self-concern alone. It is not easy to soften and have a gentle appreciation for life, no matter what we are experiencing. Still, when you are able to soften, you naturally have sympathy for yourself and others, too. You can see they are the same, with the same problems and the same promise. You are being a person to yourself, and when you are, you know how to be a person to the other, too. You may be talking to another person about your fuel pump, politics, or the weather. You may be laughing together, passing in a grocery aisle, or disagreeing wholeheartedly. But if your heart is joyful and a little sad, the bond between you and others is always there.

Whatever tradition you are studying, Chögyam Trungpa said, if it is a path with heart that you are on, then you are on an endless journey of discovering personal aloneness and falling in love with the world at the same time. In Shambhala, compassion naturally arises when you stay in touch with your joy and sadness simultaneously. This allows you to communicate in a way that's genuine and true. In this way a joyful-sad heart provides fuel to go forward in your life. The analogy Chögyam Trungpa used was as if there were a kite on a string with a hook on its end, and the hook was attached to your heart. The wind that moves the kite represents the world's energies. The kite is your own longing to communicate. And the hook in your heart is appreciation for this world. The higher the kite sails, the more it moves in the wind, the more you experience your heart. This increases your longing, which is not bad news, sorrow, or a complaint. The movement of the world's energies uplifts your heart. The world's beauty pulls you up, so this sadness isn't grief. It isn't sentimental. It isn't even very sad—just slightly sad, as if the world's energies were touching you directly, and it hurt a little bit. This makes you tender. In all traditions of human goodness this tenderness is not a flaw. It is how humans *should* feel.

Ironically, the more familiar you become with experiencing joy and sadness together, the more playful and humorous you are able to be with your kids, your housemate, your boss, the people who work for you, and the clerks at the local coffee shop. Each time you remember your genuine heart of sadness, you discover that life is more than what appears on the surface. There are endless energies in you and in trees, bankers, spouses, cars, squirrels, the soil, the morning mist, thoughts you have, and everything in you and beyond you. This makes you joyful and positive, which is the kite, and also tender and sad, which is your heart being pulled by the string on the kite that's hooked into your heart. The higher the kite sails in the wind, the more you experience your heart. The more you experience your heart, the more this increases your understanding and strength.

There is no end to this journey. Over time your heart becomes strong enough to withstand a breeze, a storm, or even a typhoon. For the fully accomplished person, no matter what life brings, you have a heart that is strong and open and feels a bond with other human beings.

PART TWO

Settling Down With Ourselves

·■·

5

Settling Down With Ourselves

·■· ·■· ·■·

Ground: All beings have the capacity to *just be* as they are.

Path: Meditating in this way.

Fruition: We increase our resourcefulness and strength.

IN order to be able to have courage and not lose heart as you go through the nit and grit of life, first of all you need to be able to settle down with yourself as you are. This takes meditative discipline. For example, the Q'ero Indians live in villages at seventeen thousand feet in the High Andes of Peru. They meditate as they go about their day, except that what they are doing is not called meditation. A Peruvian friend says that when the Q'ero see someone stopping their activity, sitting down, and looking out to the horizon from the mountain tops, they say, "Hey, look at

Americo! He's doing his thing!" He's not doing anything special. He's just being.

Just being for the Q'ero Indians is not a special activity. But for us it takes courage because there is a tendency in our culture to veer away from *just being*. We emphasize being productive, improving, achieving, or gaining something that we don't have. So in the process of living life and staying busy, we tend to lose track of our natural being and strength. Sometimes even stopping our activity for a moment produces tremendous anxiety just to be. Yet for the Q'ero Indians looking out over the mountains and for you and me, the purpose of meditation is the same—to investigate what and how our being is at the moment, to renew our strength, and to develop personal courage based on what we find.

Meditation means to *become familiar* with something. For example, when you meditate on an object or an issue, you become familiar with its ins and outs. You have a desired result that you hold in your mind. You meditate on what's puzzling you, and you look at it from different angles in order to resolve the puzzle in your mind. When your meditation has a specific focus, object, or theme like this, it is called *conditional meditation*. As you resolve the issue, your meditation ends.

There is also *unconditional meditation*, which is meditating without an object, meditating without a theme. This is meditating as becoming familiar with *just being*. It is *nothing special* meditation, as the Q'ero do. This is the basis of traditional Buddhist and Shambhala meditation. Here meditation is a deepening process, not a linear one. You aren't advancing toward anything at all. It's not like you are going from a specific condition to a specific result, from Kansas City to Boston, or from your front door to your garage. You aren't going anywhere, and the meditation never ends. You are advancing *here*, on the spot. It is called "practice," but it is not like practicing the piano or sports for a later performance. You aren't practicing for later. You are practicing to be yourself *now*. The logic is that meditation is intrinsic to human beings. As a human being you have a natural disposition just to be. Horses, dogs, birds, cats, fleas, and other beings have a natural disposition just to be, and human beings do, too.

Unconditional meditation is more advanced than meditating on an object or a theme. It is more like becoming familiar with something you already have. It's as if you have always had the capacity to meditate, like sneezing or being yourself, and somehow you forgot. Then someone says, "Do it like this—you can do it." You try it, and it works.

Although it is a deepening process, it is not necessarily having "deep experiences." Your experience just is what it is, and you are simply settling down with yourself as you are. There is nothing to be lost, nothing to be gained. You just practice being yourself in a straightforward way. Your exertion is in order to *be*. This is simple because you are just being yourself here in this moment, genuine and true. At the same time, it's also challenging because you discover you have to unravel a lot of stuff that is keeping you from being straightforward, present, genuine, and true. Meditating unconditionally is a process of opening up to understand more of the world's actual energies, including your own. You discover that unconditional meditation is a method to understand very clearly your confusion, your wisdom, how your body and mind hang together, how and when they disconnect, how your perception works, what's happening in the situation around you, what other people are feeling, and as much about your existence and your world as you want to explore.

If you look at how your intelligence works in everyday experience, it is a process of going out and coming back. You are aware very simply, and then your focus goes out, and then it comes back in. Something catches your attention, and your intelligence goes out. You try to ground yourself in a task, an activity, watching a bird bathing in a birdbath, or the meaning of a glance. When this doesn't ground you, you come back in to being simply yourself, and then you go back out again. You look for ground, which you don't find, so you come back in. Go out. It doesn't work. Come back. Go out in the environment in a different way. No ground. Come back.

This is natural, and we do it all the time. We focus, expand, let go, reason, scrutinize, select, wander, and come back while we stir an omelette or drive up to a tollbooth. In between these processes of mind there are uncontrived moments that we don't seem to control, where we come back in, relax, gain perspective, refresh ourselves, or see something that has been puzzling us in a fresh way. Each time we come back we have an opportunity to understand our heart and mind a little more.

In Shambhala and Buddhism these moments of just being that you come back to are the basis of your innate dignity. They are gaps of softness, ordinary gaps that you don't seem to control, yet they can teach you how to live your life.

Gaps of being at home with yourself are simple experiences. You are eating a pickle that comes with your sandwich, making an appointment to meet a friend, turning your car engine on, brushing your hair, thinking a thought, or not thinking at all. Whatever is going on doesn't have any complexity. Your experience and your ideas about your experience have come together in a peaceful way. Your body and mind are harmonized. Shunryu Suzuki Roshi, the Zen master, called this kind of being where your body, mind, and spirit are harmonized in one point, at the same place and time, "nothing special enlightenment." It is the basis of Zen sitting meditation and Zen meditation in action. A ninety-six-year-old friend of mine calls these gaps "blank moments" and says, "Well, dear, try to have a few." Great artists, scientists, and innovators use these experiences to harmonize their creative energies and produce the results they do. Sometimes Buddhists call these experiences of spontaneous simplicity, harmony, and clarity "no mind."

During meditation you sit down on a cushion in a quiet space and use a simple technique to bring about a mind that is settled down, open, and harmonized. Your approach is that you are not trying to do something, be good or pure, be overly focused or align yourself with something outside yourself. You are trying to be as human and natural as possible. One teacher calls it "coming home." You just come home. You are being at home with yourself. The theme is to bring together your body and mind in one particular moment, which is *this* moment, now.

There is a Sufi story about a child who asks his mother who his father is. The mother takes him on a long journey to meet his father. They go through meadows, forests, into open clearings, up steep hills. They experience changes in the weather. A day and a night pass. They experience the hot sunlight and cool moonlight. Finally they come over a hill to a house. It is the same house that they left, but the child doesn't know this. The boy is told, "Inside you'll meet your father." They enter, and the child has an experience of wonder and gratitude at meeting his father. The mother later explains to the child that as each of us goes out into the world, we make a big journey to come back to ourselves. What is the meaning of my life? What is my purpose? What does this teaching mean?" As we make our journey into the world to find the answers, we discover that the sacredness and meaning were here all along.

When we try to trace back to find the origin of anything in our experience, we find that we make a big journey to come back to ourselves. If we try to pinpoint the origin of an experience, it doesn't really work. "It's the other person." "It's the last decade, which was so messed up." "I can't help it. It's what's going on in the industry." "It's my kids." "My parents did it to me." "Being born American made me like this." "I'm sensitive, and I've suffered." "I'm life's happy child." But if you stop and try to find the source of your troubles, your promise or your awareness, the present is all you find. It's the present mind we need to understand. We are always searching for something, but everything is here.

In meditation you are bringing awareness to the experience of basic goodness, which is happening anyway. The experience of basic goodness doesn't increase with meditation, but awareness of the experience increases, and this awareness is very beneficial. So in meditation you take your posture, sit, breathe, and be. Take your posture, sit, breathe, and be. You are being genuine and simple, as much as you can, bringing your body and mind together in the moment, over and over. You are using your body, breath, and sense of being present to relate directly with reality. "Reality" here isn't saying much. It is being aware of what's here. Good posture, sitting, breathing, being.

Doing this, you discover that having your mind and body synchronized is difficult to do. One of my teachers calls it "hard work with our heart and mind" because we tend to move away from what's happening with ourselves. All the unresolved stuff you carry around from your everyday life sits down on the cushion with you. Meditating unconditionally is difficult. As you come back to the present situation again and again, you discover that it takes courage to be yourself.

You drift. If you look inward at any moment, your body is here and your mind tends to be somewhere else. Your body is in Chicago, and your mind is in California. Your body is eating a sandwich, and your mind is on the chips. Your body is in the kitchen, and your mind is in the car. It happens very fast. Moment to moment your mind has a tendency to drift away from the present. At the same time the human mind has an instinct toward being present because we are naturally curious and sensitive to what's happening now.

You can see this in everyday life. You can see yourself pull back from the moment, try to understand what is happening, ignore what is happening, open up, expand your senses, bring yourself back to what's happening, and then drift again. This goes on continually for each of us as we put on our clothes, inspect our fingernails, have an argument, eat breakfast, do our jobs, and listen for the sound of a "ping" in our car. We open. We drift. We bring ourselves back. We open. We drift again. We bring ourselves back. Usually the experience of being present and open is brief and unpredictable before your mind veers away again—trying to understand what is happening, connecting things, examining, moving closer, moving on.

The practice of meditation takes this natural process of being present, drifting, and coming back and works with it. It highlights the process, so you can see how your energies work and use the awareness to settle down and be present all the time. Meditating in this way is skillful because it's not made up. It's being what you are. Whether you are a beginner or advanced, the practice is the same—just to be. The only reason it becomes advanced is because you go through a process of undoing and unraveling layers and layers of stuff that is covering up what's there—being here and being real.

It is beneficial to relate with reality. The practice of being in the present, again and again, as much as you can, is powerful because life is powerful. Even though it can be irritatingly simple, you can gain strength from meditating because you are relating to life's energies directly rather than hiding from them. In the process of just being, you begin to pick up clues about yourself and your world. Your perceptions begin to become very clear, and your intelligence is sharpened. You begin to perceive patterns of sanity and wisdom in you and around you. And you start to perceive and go beyond the problems you find in yourself and in the culture.

In my experience, meditation is beautiful, humbling, empowering, humorous, irritating, strengthening, and slightly ironic all at once. When I first began to sit, I realized that I had enough daring and strength to sit down with anyone except myself. I was afraid of what I would find if I looked closely at myself. Somehow I thought that if I could live life faster, harder, more intensely, maybe I could get away from me. When that didn't work, I tried to outfox myself by putting up a kind of mental stop sign to slow things down that way. That only made things worse, so finally I felt I had to look into the situation. After receiving meditation instruction from Trungpa Rinpoche, finally I began to sit. There were very few resources available to support study and practice at that time, so I moved to a small Buddhist meditation center in Vermont in order to learn how to settle down with myself. I was part of a small group of practitioners living in a farmhouse, managing the land and house, studying Buddhism, trying to meditate, and constantly getting on one another's nerves. The winters were especially claustrophobic.

The more I sat and looked a little closely at my experience, the wilder my mind seemed to become. There is an analogy for this process of learning to meditate. At the beginning you look at your mind and discover it's like a monkey. It jumps around all over the place, acting frivolous and crazy. Still, you maintain your sense of dignity and continue to meditate. One day you take a closer look. Now you realize your mind is more powerful than you thought. You thought it was a monkey. It's not a monkey at all—you've got a crocodile on your knee! This crocodile is fierce, stronger than you ever imagined. One flap of its tail can knock your senses out.

A friend I had known earlier came to visit me in Vermont. I was sure he'd notice the wild and ferocious crocodile I had discovered inside myself. Instead he said, "Wow, you've changed! What is this place? Some kind of spa?" He saw composure and harmony in me. I felt like I had been riding a wild crocodile, while he saw someone who had worked to befriend herself.

Obviously meditation is difficult, or everyone would be doing it. But fundamentally meditation is a friend because it teaches you what you need to know. You may be broke, rich, loved, or forgotten by your friends, but regardless of your situation you can be a visionary human being. You can understand yourself better and understand your landlord, your grocery clerk, the people who work with you, your relatives, the birds in your yard, where your fear comes from, where others' fear comes from, and what you need to learn in life. All this comes from the simple process of sitting down with yourself.

The biggest obstacle to meditation is the idea of meditation. There's a tendency to think that meditation is a different state of mind than our everyday state of mind. We habitually think that there is something we are supposed to be experiencing that we are not experiencing. "Am I doing it now? Is this it? Should I be breathing like this? Should I be thinking these thoughts?" We drift and come back, and when we come back, we drift off again. "This is bad. This is good. This can't be it. Maybe tomorrow when I sit, I'll be able to meditate." What is in the way is the idea that resting with your ordinary mind *as it is* is not genuine enough. You need to bring that struggle to the cushion, too—as one more struggle that takes you away from being as you are, directly, in the present, now.

Unconditional meditation is the opposite of struggling to experience something pure or perceive something special. You are not trying to destroy your nightmare or build up your bliss.

The purpose is not to dwell on a particular state of mind. It is to be, in a simple and straightforward way, with the everyday beauty, boredom, tension, joy, lethargy, and speed. You have thoughts of your relatives, your coworkers, the driver who cut you off yesterday, the driver who cut you off ten years ago, your sense perceptions, sounds from the neighborhood, what you want to eat for dinner, how you don't like brussels sprouts, pain in your legs, how you are going to be a success or a failure, fears for your children, and fears for yourself. You are aware of basic dignity, an insect that has landed on your arm, thoughts of basic goodness, thoughts of how you have to do the laundry, moments of nonthought being, and anything.

No state of mind has a special charge. Everything is equal. The sound of a dog barking. Thoughts about how the neighbors should take better care of their dog. Everything is simple, accepted clearly and precisely, as it is. Trungpa Rinpoche said, "No state of mind is a V.I.P."

The foundation of meditation, the method to use, and the results to achieve are the same. The foundation is your natural disposition to be as you are, to be with your world and your experiences as they are. The method is a reminder to relax and be natural in this way. And the result is settling down with the natural processes of your body and mind, so that your human qualities of intelligence, warmth, and power can be strengthened and evolve.

6

Awake Mind

·■· ·■· ·■·

Ground: Mindfulness and awareness belong to human beings.

Path: By practicing peacefulness and insight.

Fruition: Intrinsic mindfulness-awareness unfolds
as wisdom in our life.

IN Buddhism and Shambhala *mindfulness meditation* is the
practice of bringing your mind fully into the present and stabi-
lizing yourself there. You can do this because mindfulness is
unconditional. It is intrinsic, innate, and natural for human
beings to be in the present in a simple and direct way, so the practice cultivates this. You bring your mind to the present 100 percent as you lift a cup, brush your hair, form sounds in your throat,
look at another person, punch a volleyball, or pull up your socks.

You press your mind, like your nose against a mirror, against the world with everything you do and with any perception you have.

There is a Chinese folktale about a wise old fox crossing a river that is covered with ice. The wise old fox is completely alert and inquisitive. It discriminates precisely and carefully each sound it hears, each crack in the ice, and each step of its paws. The fox feels where the ice is thin and thick and senses whether the wind is bringing a thaw or another frost. Nearby a young fox is crossing the river, too. But the young fox doesn't take the time to feel anything very much, so it crashes through and gets its tail wet.

In mindfulness meditation you are trying to be like the wise old fox—mindful of everything equally, without judgment. You are trying to do this directly, without using very much concept. The practice is to be mindful without bias for or against anything, just as basic goodness doesn't have a bias for or against. Instead, you are trying to be present directly, fully, with everything, twenty-four hours a day, without picking or choosing, as much as you can.

This practice is called *acceptance* or *the development of peace*. You are becoming at peace with yourself, slowing down, looking at and accepting the present situation. Being at peace doesn't mean being wimpy or weak. It means being realistic, calming down, not making distinctions, accepting. The present situation is what is important, so you are cultivating being realistic, calm, and even in order to be more fully present. You are looking at the details of what is happening in your body, speech, and mind and not getting caught in thinking, or trying to be different than you are, or trying to be somewhere else.

Mindful as you get up to meditate. Mindful on the cushion. Mindful as you go to the store, have a conversation, and figure out your bills. You pay attention to all the intricacies of how you move about and what you feel, what you say, what others are saying, the mood in a room, the sound of wind in the trees, how you react to someone's cough or tone of voice, how thoughts tear you away from being present, the textures and colors in your sense perceptions. You let go of the thoughts that pull you away from being fully here. Your purpose is to feel, hear, see, taste, and experience very clearly and tactually everything that happens to you.

This may sound like too much to keep track of, but in practice it's not. In reality mindfulness brings a sense of ease and precision. The more mindful you are in the present, the more well-being you feel. This comes from slowing down and learning to relax with yourself. You are beginning to appreciate life by taking out your impulse to react to your projections. This cultivates your inner strength.

At the meditation center in Vermont, we used to get flies out of the kitchen in the summers by organizing "fly brigades." We would open the door and windows, get a group of volunteers together, and have everyone wave towels from one end of the kitchen. Then we'd slowly move forward across the room to shoo the flies outside. This worked well except in the fall, when flies start to get very sleepy with the cold and coming winter and barely move at all. In the fall the flies would ride the airwaves from our towels like they were drunk. If we stopped flapping, they would hang in the cold air for a long moment and then settle down in the kitchen again. It took a lot of effort to get them from the room. During these fly brigades you could easily see their little wings and little legs and how they work. This made an impression on me. I thought, "My thoughts are like these flies. I can't really get rid of them with all this meditating, but when they slow down and hang in space, before they settle in again, I can see how they operate." A transition in meditation practice has a similar evolution to these fly brigades. You bring yourself into the present over and over, until mindfulness starts to seep into your actions and slow your impulses down. Like the cold flies hanging in the fall air, your stream of thoughts becomes slowed down and more transparent.

From this slowed-down place of seeing your thoughts more clearly, you begin to notice the environment more, and all its ins and outs. A traditional analogy for this is walking in a mist. You are practicing mindfulness and you don't realize its effect, just as when you are walking in a mist you don't realize you're getting wet. Then at some point your clothes are sopping, and you realize you're soaked. When you are soaked in mindfulness, you look around. You see that the world exists on its own, in its own way, independent of your commentary. This is a breakthrough, although nothing in particular has changed. You've just soaked yourself in mindfulness, but the result is a shift. You shift your approach from being mindful of only your own thoughts toward discovering and experiencing something new. You notice the environment around you. You can see the world in a fresh way. You can look around and see the panorama. You are gaining perspective. This is a further stage of meditation called *awareness*. It is not a linear achievement, as if awareness were next in a series of meditation steps. It's a spontaneous deepening or opening up and opening out. Like mindfulness, awareness is intrinsic. It doesn't come from meditation—it comes from being human. Meditating unconditionally simply cultivates intrinsic awareness and brings it out.

Awareness is a further stage of meditation because you are no longer preoccupied solely with yourself and what you know. From the development of acceptance, peace and not struggling, you are able to relax more and learn from the situation around you. You can understand others better, engage more fully, and enjoy what's in front of you. Enjoy doesn't mean pleasure necessarily. It means that things are lighter and more transparent. Because things are lighter, you have more humor and appreciation, and more room to move around. You can see the ins and outs and innuendos, the threats and ironies around you, and not be ruffled by them. Despite the world's forceful energies, when these energies come at you, they seem more transparent. You can see their causes, where they are powerful, and where they are weak. You see that you have options, that despite the energies coming at you, you don't have to sacrifice your dignity and strength.

Once Trungpa Rinpoche was asked what he'd do if he were kidnapped. He said, "I'd make the kidnappers laugh. That would lighten things up." Mindfulness doesn't give you a chance to lighten things up because you're working so much with the details of your sense perceptions. But awareness does because you're going deeper into the present situation, and the situation can teach you what you need to know. The more you perceive and examine how your mind works, that much more you are able to bring body and mind together as one unit to encounter and learn from a situation. Awareness is an expansion of mindfulness. It is called *mindfulness-awareness* or *insight* because you are able to see what's happening in the environment around you. Usually when we enter a space we aren't aware of who is there, the mood, the sounds, what's happening with others, the meanings and innuendos, because we are so concerned with our own agenda and what others think of us. But when you have learned to relax your sense of struggle, you can see with a fresh eye. Your intelligence has room to expand, because there is no agenda in your mind. You can see the causes and patterns in events, why someone is angry, what isn't being spoken, and what's happening in the room. If another person describes a situation to you, and you weren't there, nonetheless you can sense the dynamic, what people felt, and why they did what they did because you have learned to notice things beyond yourself. You can read the world's code.

Awareness is more advanced and subtle than mindfulness, but it's important to understand what all the great teachers in all the great traditions stress: awareness is not foreign or exotic. It is your birthright, your essence. Awareness *belongs* to human beings. Awareness *is* human beings. Therefore at any moment of your life the whole process of meditation is happening, although you may not see it, have confidence in it, or fully use it. The great teachers in the great traditions may describe meditation as a practice and a process, but increasing your awareness is not a linear thing. It is an unfolding and expanding, a going-beyond of what seems to limit you. Although you go through stages of increasing your understanding, when you connect with meditation you are not going anywhere. You are uncovering and blossoming what's always been there. Therefore your understanding *deepens* the farther that you go.

The goal of mindfulness-awareness is not to create a perfect life but to appreciate what's going on in a whole situation, so you can be more insightful, spontaneous, and engaged in what you do. As you are able to incorporate more of the world's actual energies, this builds up your strength. As you progress in your practice, you begin to gain a confident awareness about what it is to be human and how to be a human being. This is how the idea of wisdom enters in.

Even just being curious about yourself begins to build up your dignity and strength. Mindfulness is the practice, and peace and acceptance are the theme—free from struggle, and settling in. With a little practice this evolves into clear perception and confident awareness about being a human being. This is the beginning of wisdom, which comes from opening to being in the present without obstruction. The more your intelligence can expand, the more confident you become about yourself. This is a constant process and hard work because it is a process of unrav-

eling what's in the way. At the same time it's simple because it is
not self-improvement. It is a natural process of releasing the natural intelligence in you. A traditional analogy is as if you are
waking up from being asleep. The result is *awake mind*.

The first time Trungpa Rinpoche asked his students to sit a
thirty-day meditation session, we thought he was crazy. He
wanted us to sit and meditate for thirty days? But we were in
Vermont, knee-deep in commitment, and so we did. There were
about twenty of us doing this. One of the few things I remember,
besides breaking down in unconsolable sobs one night, and
besides a friend falling asleep sideways and hitting the gong that
we used to signal a session's end, was that one day I made up a
joke. It popped into my head during sitting, and it was funny.
This had never happened before, and it has never happened
since. It goes like this. "What did the Tibetan lama say when he
saw Lady Godiva ride by on her horse?" "Sam yak, sam bodhi!"
You have to know that Tibetans have animals called yaks, and
samyaksambodhi is a Sanskrit word for utter, complete enlightenment or utter, complete awake. I told my joke at teatime. In
the laughter that followed and the joyful-sadness in our situation
that we all felt, I began not to take attaining a perfect meditation
so seriously. There is no such thing as achieving perfect meditation. Instead, you are wearing out the idea of meditation.

At some point, with patience and humor, you do wear out the
heavy, opaque quality in your thoughts. Your wisdom starts to
evolve, not because you are blossoming inward so much as you are
blossoming out. You have covered so much inner ground that
now you can be enlightened by what's around you. You've gone
deeper into the situation, so you are more in touch with reality.
Now you have more capacity to help yourself and someone else.
Mindfulness-awareness practice is an endless journey of learning
to be a complete human being. Because it is not linear but deeper

into the present moment, the process is guaranteed to take you where you need to go.

Here's an example of the process taking you where you need to go. At the meditation center in the summers we used to pick cabbage worms off the cabbages by hand and transport the worms away so we wouldn't kill them. One summer day I was wearing a beautiful purple outfit that was colorful, with pants loose enough for gardening and a tight-fitting top. Trungpa Rinpoche was at the center, giving a weeklong seminar. I was working in the garden, picking cabbage worms, not thinking of very much. Then I looked up. Rinpoche was in a car in the driveway, only yards away, looking and smiling at me. It caught me by surprise. I felt completely exposed, naked, seen. Without thinking, I slammed myself down to the ground, right into the vegetable patch. It happened very fast. There I was in my purple outfit, lying in the dirt.

The warmth of his smile was overwhelming. I had seen myself as beautiful in the summer sunlight, and he did, too. And now there I was, flat on the ground, my nose inches from the dirt. Once I was down, I was shocked at my action. What would he think of this new student of his? I decided, "I'll pretend I'm picking cabbage worms off the plants from this angle." So I lay there on my stomach in the garden, with big green cabbages above my head, picking worms for what seemed like a long-enough time for him to go away. At one point I got up a little to check, and he was still there, leaning out the car window. Only now he was really grinning at me. I ducked back down again. I felt stupid and phony picking cabbage worms from this position, and yet I was grateful the little worms were there with me. Then it dawned on me that just like in meditation practice this, too, was mindfulness! And a bigger awareness hit me. I was aware of the magnitude, power, and ordinariness in the moment. I recognized I was sharing something together with my teacher, feeling a sense of love and not being able to handle it. Then I realized that even being flattened in the vegetable patch *was* handling it, and I felt a huge humor and warmth.

We never talked about it, but I learned something in the garden that day about awareness and the human heart. I had shock and a sudden impulse, which sent me down, wham, among the cabbages. I had a sense of shared beauty and love, genuine mindfulness picking those little worms, and then paranoia, tenderness, humor, importance, humility, because the whole situation was rich with meaning, extra-ordinary, and also ridiculous. Insight into the situation kept unfolding for me. A big awareness! If I were there now in my purple outfit, if I had it to do over again, knowing what I know, maybe I would just look at him and share the recognition of being open in the same moment, and let it be. Maybe I would be able to stabilize the awareness of sharing a bond of love a little bit. Nothing else would really change. In that moment I realized, as I still do today, "This meditation thing is teaching me." Unconditional meditation helps unfold our nature and goodness as human beings. Once we are on a personal journey, it unfolds as growing wisdom in our life.

7

How to Meditate

▪ ▪ ▪

Ground: Adopting an attitude of dignity.

Path: We train our body, speech, and mind in simplicity.

Fruition: This lays a good foundation for our humanity to unfold.

IN Akira Kurosawa's film *Kagemusha: The Shadow Warrior* there is a medieval battle scene filmed from a cliff above the plains where a fight between two clans is taking place. A great warrior and his generals are seated on the cliff so they can see and be seen by their troops. In the scene the great warrior is a "shadow warrior," an imposter chosen by the clan's leaders because he looks like the true warrior. No one but the inner circle knows that the true warrior has died. This shadow warrior is a gentle peasant with a big heart. From time to time he gasps as he watches the carnage of dying men and dying horses on the plains beneath him. Each time he gasps, the generals command him, "Hold, hold." He composes himself, then he gasps again. They say, "Hold, hold." It's a fabulous scene. He sits there choicelessly with his soft and gentle heart and also an attitude of strength, stillness, balance, and command.

When you take your seat in meditation, you are like this shadow warrior. Your approach is that you are a dignified person. You are sane, regal, and worthwhile as you are, and it is fully natural for you just to sit and be with an open heart. Your attitude is not to escape what's happening, but to get into it. Your intention is to open your senses, engage fully in what you're doing, and proclaim your sanity. You have taken your seat and adopted a sense of command, like a great warrior taking your seat on a battlefield. There is a meditation phrase called *taking your seat,* and you can use this image of the great warrior to remember it.

The most important meditation instruction is to have the attitude or view that you are sitting like a monarch. You are claiming your authority. You have gained perspective. You are in command of your life. This doesn't mean you are being fierce or stoic, or trying very hard. You are just sitting down on a chair, on a cushion, on the floor, on this earth, and being yourself. The traditional analogy for the meditation cushion is an imperial seat. The strength is that you are removing yourself from your ordinary concerns, bringing stillness and balance to your body and awareness to your mind. You aren't *doing* anything. You are simply making a statement of strength.

In Shambhala this view is also called having *good head and shoulders.* It is something more than a good external posture. It is a statement about your dignity—that no situation can overwhelm you. Your strength is what guides you. Your view is immoveable, that you have what you need—a firm body, a wakeful mind, and an open heart. Your view is immoveable. You can be wounded, insulted, threatened, confused, crushed, sobbing, but you can't be talked out of your dignity because it's so much a part of you. Some Zen teachers call this style *soft front, hard back*. In Zen archery it is called *strong mind, soft heart, and shooting dignity*. It is your attitude or view.

Body

WHEN you sit down to meditate with this view, you are working with three aspects of your being. Each corresponds to a natural process of body, speech, and mind. The first is to acknowledge and appreciate a still and balanced body. Find a place to meditate where you won't be disturbed. This could be in your bedroom, your study, a workshop you have, a public meditation hall—any place where you can remove yourself from your usual activity and sit in an ordinary and simple way. If you use a cushion on the floor, sit in the center of the cushion and establish a good balance so that you feel well sat. You can keep a meditation cushion for this purpose. Sit cross-legged in a simple way, legs crossed at the ankles. Another method is to use a comfortable straight-backed chair and maintain good posture as much as you can. Here your legs are not crossed, the soles of your feet touch the floor, and you don't rely unnecessarily on the chair to maintain an upright posture.

Rest your hands with palms open facing down on your thighs. Make your back straight, with your chin slightly tucked in, so the vertebrae in the back of your neck are aligned with your spine. This way your head is balanced and your neck isn't tilted out of alignment with the rest of your spine. Feel your hips, shoulders, and head aligned and your weight balanced on both hips. Let your elbows fall straight down from your shoulders. Don't have your shoulders rounded forward or strained. Relax your jaw.

Now you can pull yourself up into a statement of good head and shoulders. Feel your lower back, which will be somewhat curved in. Feel your upper back, your shoulders, your neck. An analogy is that your vertebrae are like gold coins placed on top of one another and perfectly aligned so that the golden coins of your spine are perfectly stacked. When you feel yourself aligned with good head and shoulders in this way, then you can relax and settle in. The ideal situation in meditation is where you have the most balance and harmony.

This seated posture is sometimes referred to as a *royal pose.* You feel like a monarch, fully legitimate. You are seated on this earth, surveying your world. Your eyes are open because you are not daydreaming or falling asleep. You are acknowledging, "This is my world, so be it." Your gaze is relaxed, and somewhat down—resting in the space four to six feet in front of you. The gaze of your eyes is relaxed because you are not trying to pull in visual data. Instead, you are at ease. The entire attitude is one of openness, dignity, letting go, and letting be. You are able to maintain yourself as things in your life come and go. All this concerns instruction for the *body.*

Breath

BREATH corresponds to the principle of *speech*, which is the energy of communication and flow in your life. Breath is how you survive and exist. It is the continuity of life and your communication with a larger world. The meditation instruction is to be mindful of your breath. Your breath naturally comes in and goes out without obstruction when your body is aligned. Identify with your breath as it is. Feel your natural breath. Be the breath. Let your mouth be very slightly open so your breath can move naturally without being obstructed.

There are many techniques for using the breath. You can be mindful of your breath going in and out, or you can be mindful of your out-breath alone. When you are mindful of the out-breath alone, you can practice it like this. When the breath goes out, go along with it simply. Breath goes out, you go out. Breath dissolves, you dissolve. As you breathe out, you diffuse. In-breath is a gap in the basic flow of expanding out. Out, dissolve. Out, dissolve. Just let in-breath occur without too much attention. You are using a gentle emphasis on the out-breath to build trust in a natural state of meditation, trusting in a natural state of mind.

You can also practice being mindful of your in-breath and out-breath equally, in order to develop mindfulness of body and strengthen your sense of being here. When you meditate in this way, the result is to be more grounded in your body, in the present moment, here on the earth. This may be what you need to stabilize your mind, to stay in the meditation situation long enough to absorb and understand something, and not to let sense perceptions and discursive thoughts tear you away. When you practice being mindful in this way, maintain your sense of body-mindfulness and put your attention lightly on your breath equally as it comes in and goes out.

Breathing is a natural activity. With either breathing technique you are doing the same thing—assuming a dignified sitting posture and identifying with your breath as you begin to make friends with yourself in a fundamental sense. You are trying to be present on the spot, and you are using your natural breath to do this. Your body becomes breathing. Your mind becomes body and breathing. The practice is to go along with this situation simply, using the breath to be present, as much as you can. The body is happening now. The breath is happening now. When you start to move away from being present, come back simply to your posture and your breath.

Mind

As you practice in this way, you will become aware of your thinking process. We have covered body and speech. Now this is the third principle, the natural process of *mind*. In the practice of mindfulness of body and breath, thinking is accommodated very simply, as thinking. You are not shocked by your thoughts. You are not thrilled or disgusted by your thoughts. You are like a mountain, and thinking is like weather on the mountain. It comes and goes while the mountain stays steady, immovable, and peaceful. Thinking becomes superficial. When you notice you are thinking, use a light touch to bring yourself back to the posture, back to the breath. You notice that you are thinking, then back to the posture, back to the breath. Whatever your thoughts are, whether they are exotic, boring, lustful, or thoughts about how you need to eat more vegetables, the content doesn't matter. Thinking is just thinking. This way nothing that comes up is ignored, and nothing is highlighted or exaggerated either. If you want to make love to your neighbor, it is thinking. If you want to kill your neighbor, it is thinking. If you want to invent a new gadget, do the laundry, or eat a piece of pie, it is thinking. No grand schemes—just the naturalness of being here. Simply note thoughts and feelings, your basic discursiveness, and return to your posture and breath. Return to your view that thinking is thinking, and use the breath to come back.

Big thoughts, little thoughts, important thoughts, nasty

thoughts, flat thoughts, colorful thoughts—just come back over and over to being here. You can mentally label the big thoughts— the ones that take you out of the room—as "thinking," and just notice the other ones. Overall, the most important guidelines for mindfulness training are precision, gentleness, and letting go.

This practice is called *touch and go*. Thinking, breath, and body are natural processes that occur. You touch them, and then let go of them, over and over. This is powerful because the flow of life is powerful. Touch and go allows you to see clearly and accurately. Also, it is a method for developing your courage. You are brave to touch your thoughts, whatever they are, and then brave to let go of them. You have body, breath, and mind, and mind is the principle of openness or space. You are working with mind and body together, not with mind alone, so you never leave reality. Everything is unified by your posture and your view. Thoughts come and go, and you settle in.

As you meditate, the intrinsic mindfulness-awareness in you becomes highly strengthened. This is what you are trying to ground yourself in. And to your surprise, it works. When you sit down to meditate, you may be rattled by your mind and body going at different speeds with different purposes. Yet when you get up from meditation, somehow you're more unified and dig- nified. You can be yourself in a lighter, more realistic and humor- ous way. You are more intelligent. You have more wisdom.

There is no such thing as an ideal meditative state. The pur- pose is not to cultivate a particular state of mind but to accom- modate what's happening without judgment, so you can see what's there. Your time on the cushion may be dark and chaotic, or it may be clear, high, and insightful. Whatever you experience, the approach is, "This is meditation. I am sane. Basic goodness is real. Basic goodness is the ultimate solidity. I am brave and dig- nified. The earth is my witness to this."

It depends on your life situation and circumstances, but it is good to develop some kind of daily contact with meditation. Try short periods when your mind is clear. That way you have a chance to tune in to the naturalness of being as you are. Try this many times. Also be willing to sit when your mind is a mess. Meditate when you are happy, when you are sad, when you are busy, and when you are bored. Sometimes you will have the opportunity to practice meditation, and not the desire. Sometimes you will have the desire to practice meditation, and not the opportunity. Do what you can. But when the desire and opportunity come together, you should practice! Maybe ten to twenty minutes is enough. You could meditate in the morning and in the evening. Maybe five minutes several times a day is all you can do. That's good. When you have time, you can meditate for longer. And it's important to receive personal instruction if you can.

With the practice of meditation you are trying to make your mind flexible enough to reexamine yourself and your world. You are taming the wildness of your mind so you can experience yourself and your world directly. How you do anything—how you relate to your mind, how you relate to your body, and what kind of action it creates when you go beyond yourself—is very powerful and has an effect on yourself and others. In meditation practice you are trying to make the mind open and subtle enough to see how perception works, who you are, what's happening around you, and what your purpose is so you can use your senses without judgment, give your humanity an opportunity to come out more, and engage with your world.

8

The Commentator and the Cocoon

·■· ·■· ·■·

Ground: Just seeing the commentator and cocoon.

Path: Begins to weaken their strategy.

Fruition: And produce sympathy toward ourselves and others.

SOMETIMES we have to meditate to even realize that we *are* thinking. Sometimes when we first sit, it can seem like sitting only makes us think more, but what is increasing is our awareness that we are thinking. Now we can discover how much everything in our everyday life is made up of our thinking!

Morning dawns. The alarm goes off, or you wake up to the early-morning sounds of birds or cars. It is still dark outside, or you see the morning light. You hear the birds chirp, the refrigerator gurgling, somebody stirring. You feel the cool morning air of an open window or a lowered thermostat. You hear the morning newspaper being delivered, or the cabs and trucks as the city starts to wake up. You are awake, open and fresh.

Or morning dawns. And somewhere in the open space, something goes wrong with your mind. It starts to talk to you. "This isn't going to be a good day. Here comes anxiety. It is never going to go away. I am not up to doing motherhood, fatherhood, marriage, or my job. Even my car doesn't look so good anymore. This day will not go so well. The television program last night was sort of funny. Still, on the whole I'm sick of television. Something in my life should be happening that isn't happening. Maybe I should change the kind of tea I drink. I'll do things a little differently today. That might help."

Or morning dawns. "This is going to be a great day. I know what I want to accomplish. I'll lose a few pounds, get a new computer, have a conversation with my kids about school. Sure, I have some hurdles to jump over, but I have a rough idea of what to do next. At least I am giving life a shot. I've always done that. That's what I like about myself. I have a lot of determination. Whatever happens, I'm up for it. What a day!"

Or morning dawns. You take a shower and go through your morning routine. Things feel wholesome, good, neutral. You know how to ride the flow of your life. You feel okay—confident, healthy, capable. Then you turn on the morning news program, or the phone rings and you answer it, or you sit down to have breakfast with your kids or your partner. *You're* okay, and out of the blue *they* step into *their* habitual storylines, just like you step into yours! It shocks you a little, then you jump into their current so you can fit into society and begin your day.

In these cases what is happening is that your horizon is shrinking. Your sense perceptions are starting to be blocked. Pretty soon you are washing your face, and you can't smell the soap. You are eating your breakfast, and you can't taste the toast. You don't even feel the phone against your ear. You open the door to go outside and can't experience the freshness. It doesn't take long before you have no idea what you are doing. You lose track of how you are thinking and even that you *are* thinking. You are slowly putting yourself into a smaller world. Shambhala calls this discovering *the commentator* and *the cocoon.*

When a caterpillar weaves a cocoon, it produces strands and strands of sticky stuff. The caterpillar crisscrosses, changes route, and lays the sticky stuff down in patterns to create a safe, snug, secure home where no light can come in, where no breeze, nothing unpredictable, nothing unfamiliar and threatening can get in from the outside. The aspect of your mind that is constantly commenting, judging, and interpreting is like this caterpillar. Your commentator thinks the same thoughts over and over, repeats the same behaviors over and over, and justifies them in the same old way, until the cocoon woven by these thoughts and behaviors feels good and natural.

We weave the cocoon out of our personal sticky stuff—our thoughts, our plans, our personality, our history, our routines, our desires and complaints—the same thoughts, about the same things, over and over. The same material is chewed and regurgitated to come to the same conclusions, over and over. Everything is interpreted in the same way. Even arguments with our mate and conversations with our friends are repetitions of the same secure thing, over and over. We talk with ourselves and have the same imaginary conversations, over and over. We come down the stairs, walk out of the house, pull out of the drive, get off the subway. Wherever we are, we look out and see the same lukewarm world we saw yesterday and the day before, over and over. We play the same lukewarm mental tapes over and over.

Trungpa Rinpoche described having a cocoon as like smelling

your own armpit. There is something in your intelligence that likes the comfortable, slightly nauseating smell of your own habitual patterns. It's always full of only *your* odors, *your* thoughts, and *your* life. It's safe and secure—so safe that nothing fresh, nothing foreign, nothing unpredictable can get in. Everything is familiar and smooth. Now you can feel comfortable and uninspired, and you can go to sleep.

You can weave a cocoon out of your job, your relationships, your laundry tasks, the evening news—anything and everything that has meaning for you can be a cocoon. I have friends who have a beautiful home in an isolated mountain area. When I first visited them, we stood on their deck admiring the view. Across a vast and gentle meadow, just short of layers of mountain ranges, if you looked closely you could see a sixth house going up among the trees. My friends turned to each other and clucked, "Another house. Look what's happening to the neighborhood!" Then we had a good laugh because living in a spacious environment like this can breed cocooning, too. Your commentator can even make depression comfortable because at least it's familiar, and it's yours. The commentator's function is to spin out what you think you need to feel comfortable and snug—combative thoughts, hungry thoughts, bored thoughts, jazzed-up thoughts, irritated thoughts, possessive thoughts, anxious thoughts, murderous thoughts, any kind of world that will make you feel at home. Its purpose is to breed a lukewarm and secure existence. But underneath you are not all that happy with the results. It's as if everything were on a dimmer switch. Nothing flows. Everything seems suffocating and superficial. There are no sharp edges anywhere. You have wrapped yourself in a fake reality. The sky over your head is stuck. The atmosphere is stuck. You feel you have real limits. Nothing is personally experienced. You feel numb, dim, blanketed down. Everything is reinterpreted and logical. Nothing matters except this little patch of real estate called me and mine, and even this looks a little bleak.

The cocoon is basically an expression of poverty. It breeds depression. Its surface is snug and familiar, but underneath you feel broke. You have no interest in your situation, no resources to deal with things, and any invitation to step into a larger world is too threatening, too exhausting, too disorienting, too subtle. You feel you will be overwhelmed. Better to stick with what you know, maintain your life as it is, and hope for the best. Better not to look up. Better to keep your life regular and secured, rather than try to go beyond yourself.

An elderly lady told me about working in a secretarial pool for the Canadian government when she was young. Two government officials worked there, separated by desks, and they couldn't get along. One man was English and the other man was Polish. Their conflict was so bad that one day the government built a wall between them. First the Englishman came around the wall and told the secretaries triumphantly, "We English people never give up!" And then the Polish man came around the wall and told the secretaries triumphantly, "We Polish people never give up!" And the secretaries said to each other, "So stupid. This doesn't make sense at all!" These two men were stuck in their cocoons. The secretaries could see that they were stuck, but the individual men couldn't see it.

Cocooning is a human thing we do. You can have your early afternoon cocoon, early evening cocoon, going to the mall cocoon, going to a meeting cocoon, eating food cocoon, going to sleep cocoon, English cocoon, Polish cocoon, never giving up cocoon, and so on. We step into a cocoon like stepping into familiar clothes, getting into a familiar car, or driving down a familiar road. It is difficult and exposing to face our cocoon, let alone get out of it. Just seeing it can be unpleasant. But the cocoon isn't a thing. There is always the possibility of stepping out of it. It's made out of nothing but our mind stitching connections together so that we can feel secure, so that we feel we "have a handle" on society, ourselves, life.

When we glimpse a larger world outside our cocoon, it throws how we are hiding into high relief. This can be quite painful but it is a good sign. I remember watching Hamlet on television and suddenly breaking out into a sweat. I never seem to sweat, but that night I did. I was cocooning in taking revenge for a relationship that didn't work out, and Shakespeare nailed me.

You can see your cocooning when something in you is irritated with hiding in your familiar patterns and longs to experience fresh air. That longing for fresh air is the beginning of having courage. From your longing you develop the possibility of not being imprisoned, and you start to move toward what you are envisioning. In the process you find that there are two sides to your intelligence. One aspect of your intelligence tries to make a home for itself in familiar fantasies. Another aspect of your intelligence is more daring, sharp, and up-to-date. This second aspect comments on your tendency toward security. It sees that a lot of what you do is trying to safeguard yourself against ambiguity, uncertainty, boredom, or just being yourself. It sees you fidget. It sees you exaggerate when you don't know how to handle yourself. It sees you dream of murderers or seek revenge when you feel inadequate to open up. Your intelligence works to modulate things so life isn't too vivid, and then it complains about the dimness! It complains that you are hiding.

The warrior's entire path involves, in an increasingly subtle way, moving toward greater courage and openness and escaping from the cocoon. This is a gradual process of learning to open our heart and mind moment to moment. It is a path of compassion. Here compassion means accepting, appreciating, warming up, having sympathy, seeing through. There's nothing wrong with our everyday activities as they are. You don't need to leave your everyday life behind. You don't need to change your activities or your experience. If you're not trying to find security, if you're not wrapping yourself in a fake reality, regardless of what you're doing, you're not cocooning.

We only need to stop hiding in patterns of thinking in order to fantasize that things are in our control. Things are not in our control. They never have been, not really, and they never will be. They just are what they are. When we are so concerned for our security, we don't even notice that we have a soft spot or a greater vision, or are suffering in a cocoon. We don't see basic goodness. We don't have compassion for fearful people, including ourselves. We don't see through the commentator, and we suffer a lot. But just seeing the cocoon begins to weaken its strategy. We begin to become a little more visionary. We begin to take a greater interest, a sympathetic interest, in a larger world.

9

Planting Seeds of Fearlessness

·■· ·■· ·■·

Ground: Fear is seemingly ubiquitous in our life.

Path: Having the courage to get to know our fear.

Fruition: We discover tenderness that is useful,
realistic, and brave.

WHAT is bothering you as you create a cocoon is fear, fear,
and more fear. All beings have fear, and human beings do, too.
You have fear of relationships, fear of being alone, fear of failing,
fear of succeeding, fear of anger, fear of losing your mind, fear of
seeing your mind, fear of not having friends, fear of having too
many friends. You fear for your children and for children on
another continent. Sometimes when you sit and open up, you are
suddenly afraid purely because you feel exposed in a new way.

Even if you manage to smooth your life into a regular and secured world, something can come along and take your security away.

You do the laundry, walk the dog, fidget, shift your posture, open the refrigerator, take a job, and develop a friend to avoid fear. Also you don't do the laundry, don't walk the dog, don't fidget, don't shift your posture, don't open the refrigerator, don't take a job, and don't develop a friend to avoid fear. The point isn't that you are a coward. It's that you are human. As human beings, you and I need, deep down, to not be afraid of ourselves. This is the essence of the warrior's practice. The Shambhala teachings are designed to help build up a strong heart and a strong mind, so you and I can go beyond our fear.

Fear is anxiety, nervousness, a sense of inadequacy, fidgeting, experiencing terror. You have fears that you can prop up with logic, like fear of losing your job, losing your property, embarrassing yourself in front of others, or fear of harm coming to the people, animals, landscape, and things you love. You can provide reasons why these fears are valid and people understand. Yet sometimes your fear doesn't have any reason. It comes out of nowhere. It just hits you.

The function of fear is to frighten you. That's its job. When it does its job, you lose your strength. You lose a sense of humor and playfulness. There is no lightness or joy in your system anymore. Your inner posture crumbles. You feel you don't have the resources you need, and you can't improvise.

Courage as a warrior depends on getting to know fear. If we ignore fear, we can't go beyond it. Trungpa Rinpoche called it a giant kindling log that we can use to develop a giant fire of fearlessness. The way to develop courage is not to cast out fear, but to find out more about it by looking directly at the fear. Until you see what the problem is, trying to get away from the fear just gives the fear more energy. Finding out more about your own fear *is* the fearlessness. It *is* the leap you need to take.

There is a story about Trungpa Rinpoche as a young man. He was the abbot of a group of monasteries in eastern Tibet, and he visited the monasteries regularly to guide administration, conduct ceremonies, and give teachings. One day he and his traveling party were approaching a monastery on foot when a vicious guard dog rushed directly at them. The other monks scattered to run away from the dog, but Rinpoche rushed straight at the dog. The dog was so startled that it stopped, turned, and ran away. Later when teaching in the West, Rinpoche gave instructions on working with fear that, like this story, involve turning directly into the fear. He taught to look at the fear. You can see it is there to frighten you. That's what it is trying to do. Keep your awareness on the fear. The awareness itself undermines the fear's strategy; then, underneath the experience of fear, you will discover tenderness. Tenderness is always there. It takes manual work, but once you have contacted your tenderness, then you can improvise.

Try it. Take a simple, ordinary fear. For example, you need to make a decision, and for whatever reason it scares you. The phone rings, and for no apparent reason you feel a flicker of fear to pick up the phone. Don't brush the fear off as insignificant. Instead, take the time to look right at it without the goal of getting rid of it. Bring your awareness to it. Now go a little deeper. Underneath the fear you can find tenderness. This tenderness is gentle, realistic, and calm—just the resources you were lacking. When you contact the tenderness, it changes the experience. Now you are contacting the strength you need. You are calm and realistic, and you can pick up clues about how to proceed. Your intelligence has room to move. You can see whether there's wisdom, or no wisdom, in picking up the phone or rushing at the dog.

This is a three-step process. Looking at your fear and just seeing its purpose is the first step of going beyond it. Its purpose is clear. The fear is trying to frighten you. The next step is to soften and respect your experience just as it is. This way you can contact the tenderness in you, which is genuine and real. This tenderness isn't weakness. It's matter-of-fact and very strong. It makes you calm because it's levelheaded and realistic. Finally, use your calmness to go into the fear. Instead of running away, instead of trying to put the fear behind you or save yourself, just trust your humanity and march in. "Hello, fear." If it seems like this is the same old fear, so be it. "I haven't seen you for months. I was wondering where you were!" If it's a new one, "Hey, I haven't met you before." The three steps are look, soften, and just march in.

There is a related story about Milarepa, the great Tibetan poet-yogi. Early in his life Milarepa's family was very badly treated by an uncle, and his mother wanted to take revenge. So Milarepa became a black magician to please his mother, and he learned a lot of negative tricks. One thing led to another, and Milarepa murdered a lot of people at the wedding party of his uncle's daughter. Now the mood in the local community changed. Before the wedding the local community had been sympathetic to Milarepa's family plight, but now people feared him. Milarepa became isolated, and he experienced remorse. Finally he went to study with a great Buddhist teacher. Eventually Milarepa spent the rest of his life in the Himalayan mountains in retreat, meditating and singing songs of realization to hunters, villagers, and retreatants, who became his students.

One day while in solitary retreat Milarepa went to gather firewood, and when he came back there were demons in his cave. He shouted at them to go away. He tried everything he knew to scare them, and some of them left. But one of the demons wouldn't leave. He threw sticks at it and tried magic spells. Nothing worked. Finally Milarepa said, "Okay, make yourself at home!

Let's sit down. We'll talk about the teachings. Make yourself comfortable, and have some nettle soup!" And the demon disappeared. Milarepa sang the demon a parting song, which you can write on a piece of paper and use as a slogan for yourself. "With compassion, I overcome the demons. All blame I scatter to the winds!" This is what we learn to do with our fear. "Tell me about yourself. I'm genuinely interested. You've come a long way to find me. Have some soup!"

When our heart is challenged, it's difficult to stay genuine and true and to befriend our problems as they are. We long to go beyond them, instead of examining them to see what the issue really is. Based on our longing, the impulse to move away from our difficulties gets triggered very fast. But Milarepa's advice is not to try to get away from experience. The warrior's discipline is to lean into what frightens you. You can open to the fear or not, and you're choosing to open up. Don't look away. Even if you are afraid, don't run away. Open to what you are feeling. Soften. Then go into the fear. When you do, you experience a shift. You may become aware of feeling cool and alone, and that sense of slightly cold aloneness makes you feel together and realistic. Now you are a 100 percent real person. You are calm from being real. Now you can use your intelligence and your heart, and improvise.

You just practiced the warrior's discipline. You went into the fear, and in the process you transcended the obstacle. You came out the other side. The process is like opening a door and going in. The threshold where you were is completely transcended and you find yourself on the other side of fear. You are strengthened and confident. Rinpoche called it a practice of *going in and coming out.* When you go into your fear instead of ignoring it, you find you are already coming out on the other side. Put your awareness in the actual feeling of being afraid. This accomplishes more than 50 percent of the shift. Then the fear dissolves, and you are left with yourself. This is the tenderness. It is a *pragmatic* tenderness. Now you can pick up clues about what to do. Just seeing the obstacle very clearly, just using awareness once you really see the obstacle, your genuine intelligence arises by itself.

The key is really in how you relate to yourself. You can't transform fear without trusting that basic goodness is in your experience. Without confidence in basic goodness, you try to step back from the fear. Now it's purely a question of who is going to win, the fear or you. This sets up a struggle, and the struggle makes you numb. Your senses shut down, which reduces your sense of life. Now you feel you don't have the resources to deal with the fear. You can throw sticks and magic spells at the fear, like Milarepa did, but this doesn't work. The fear moves in to stay.

Instead of this, the practice is to provide gentleness and hospitality for your experience. This increases your awareness, and awareness increases your intelligence and strength. Experience becomes workable. Your compassion becomes activated, and the skillfulness of your action increases too, because underneath your fear is tenderness, which is soft, calm, and somewhat visionary. Using your vision, now you can improvise how to proceed from what's happening in the environment and from directions inside yourself.

When you explore fear, where it comes from, when it arises, how it arises, what its texture is, where it goes, and so on, you are planting seeds of fearlessness in your system. Each time you invite your fear to come in closer and have some nettle soup, you plant another seed of fearlessness. The social vision of Shambhala calls the fearless experience of basic goodness the essence of a warrior's practice. In Buddhism fearlessness is described a little differently, as a proclamation of openness and generosity, but the meaning is the same—every state of mind is workable. By planting seeds of confidence in the skillfulness of your own mind, you are never trapped anywhere. This confidence plants seeds of compassion, too—because you are never trapped, no one else is either.

When you come into the present, you don't know what the outcome will be. If you regard this as an entrapment and try to run away, you dig yourself deeper into a hole you're in. But if you regard the entrapment as real, you can have an experience of resourcefulness. You find you have a pragmatic, practical, and resourceful tenderness in you, and this way your relationship with fear shifts into fearlessness. Fearlessness isn't a struggle to keep a stiff upper lip, steel your jaw, or suck it up. Fearlessness isn't heavy or teeth-grinding. It's cheerful and very light. It's having no doubts, no second thoughts—just being straightforward and open to the experience you are having.

During the last teaching Trungpa Rinpoche gave in the San Francisco Bay area, he said, "If you remember nothing that I've told you, remember this. Don't be afraid of who you are." Just being friendly to yourself puts you in contact with the world in a wakeful and inquisitive way. You are tender, but not completely tender. You are compassionate, but not idiotically compassionate. You are beginning to contact fully your resources as a human being. You can be inquisitive and resourceful as you are. If you like, you can use the image from meditation of being a great warrior taking your seat, or of having an open heart and strong posture, to help you. Having the courage to know your fear, you are able to accept challenges—and therefore you are brave.

PART THREE

Courage in Everyday Life

·■·

10

Courage in Everyday Life

▪· ·▪· ·▪·

Ground: Unconditional awareness is our nature.

Path: By unconditionally trusting our state of mind on the spot.

Fruition: We become resourceful and brave in everyday life.

WITH meditation, you discover that you are capable. You are capable of tears, capable of laughter, capable of yellow, capable of red. You are capable of murder, love, feeling great, feeling depressed, making spaghetti, and walking around the block. You are capable of being straightforward and being devious. You have the capacity to take a risk, pull up your socks, stay as you are, or change the course you're on. You discover that you have a limitless capacity purely from being a human being. Also, there's something else. You discover that you are capable of delivering yourself from some of your obstacles. You find that you are not so hot-tempered, impulsive, bored, or diffused as you used to be. You can free yourself from some of the things that bother you.

Still, when you get up from the cushion you're not all that settled in your strength. In the midst of an action you drop your confidence in being strong. You make a big distinction between practice and everyday life. Once you're on your feet, you say, "Things are fine, honest. They're good. They're great!" but they're also somewhat shaky underneath. You don't feel all that brave in your everyday life. Just dealing with your landlord and coworkers takes daring, compassion, and energy. Situations come at you, and suddenly you feel you need to break away or slow down, speed up, pull back, encourage, get involved, block, melt, see, open, let go—whatever is appropriate. Yet you forget how to go about it with any courage or dignity, or where to find the resources in yourself. It's as if you never had the capability to be strong or free at all! On the cushion you may have felt that, roughly speaking, courage and strength will be executed, probably, here in the vicinity of me, by me, when an unknown challenge comes along. But you're not all that confident in everyday life. And without a confident and definite openness to what the world presents *immediately*, right *now*, you aren't really courageous.

For years I thought Rinpoche didn't *really* mean that gentleness was the path. I thought gentleness couldn't possibly get one through life's challenges. Growing up I tried to learn to reason because my father was a scientist who challenged me and I felt I needed to toughen up. In addition, I had long conversations with myself about being brave, having backbone, about the fact that success or failure was not the point as long as I tried. But I didn't feel very brave. I seemed unusually afraid of the dark, dying, ghosts, and disappearing. When I was little, I read books under the bedcovers at night using a little clamp-on light that I could turn off if I heard my parents coming. It wasn't the reading that compelled me. I was afraid to go to sleep.

In Shambhala we can't become truly gentle without going through our fear. And we can't become truly fearless without realizing gentleness. The notion of a warrior is a person who gains all-accomplishing victory by not having any enemy. This doesn't mean you don't have any enemies or difficult relationships! It means that you don't have any doubts that awareness is your nature, so that's where you make your home, and that's what makes your victorious. This may sound very bland. You don't cling to anything that takes you away from the expansiveness of awareness, and you don't cling to awareness either. In fact, don't cling at all. This is challenging. When you brush your hair, you brush your hair with confident awareness. When you put on your socks and they don't match, you don't feel the world is out to get you. You don't have second thoughts about yourself. If you are meeting an unreasonable person, you don't feel you have to shake off the situation prematurely. In Shambhala vision this is how our courage is built up, from having fearlessness in the smallest details of everyday life, even brushing our hair or putting on our socks. Fearlessness is unconditionally being without doubts, fundamentally being cheerful and light, not having cowardice about your experience at all. When you achieve this kind of awareness in everyday life, you finally become a truly gentle and courageous human being.

Jakusho Kwong Roshi, the meditation master at Sonoma Mountain Zen Center, illuminated this for me. Once we were talking and he described vividly a disappointment he had. Suddenly Roshi stopped, his breath hung in the air, he let the disappointment be there, and then he slightly smiled at me. He was open. His disappointment hung in the air. And that was that. My experience of him was extraordinarily crisp and clean. I felt he had no doubts, no second thoughts, no extra mental commentary. I felt as if I could see Roshi's awareness burning up thoughts on the spot, that he was fully there and not clinging to anything. Chögyam Trungpa said that being with Kwong Roshi's teacher, who was also Trungpa Rinpoche's good friend, was like being with a burning tip of incense. My experience of Kwong Roshi was like that, as if his confidence was 100 percent freshly made on the spot and all the nagging doubts that usually entice us away from being fully present were freshly being set aflame.

If each of us stopped and looked at ourselves right now, if you and I went back, back and back, not in time but taking apart our individual existence in the present moment, we would find a state of being in us that has no theme, no history or memories. This is intrinsic basic goodness. When you are aware of basic goodness, you have no thought, no tricks, no scheme or plan, no limitation, and no problem or irritation anywhere. You're aware in the present moment. But contacting your basic goodness doesn't give you doubtlessness, confidence, or courage. Basic goodness is there whether you're being cowardly or brave! Individual courage only manifests when you confirm that there isn't an actual problem anywhere. As I am, there is no actual problem in my being. In brushing my hair, in relaying this disappointment, in my present state of mind, in this very moment, there is no problem in my being anywhere. This takes something more than being aware of basic goodness. It takes a warrior's discipline.

Meher Baba didn't say, "Don't worry, be happy." He said, "Being cheerful is a divine art. Don't worry, be happy." There is a big difference. "Being cheerful is a divine art" indicates a practice and discipline. Sometimes Trungpa Rinpoche called this *first thought, best thought discipline,* where "thought" stands for a state of mind that's straightforward and fresh, like a burning tip of incense that consumes itself on the spot. This may sound simpleminded and not very chic. But as a discipline it's actually very advanced. It's more than basic goodness. It's more than mindfulness-awareness, because you are confirming that you trust your being. You trust your being 100 percent, without looking for feedback that you're on track. You simply have unconditional trust in your nature as awareness on the spot. Not awareness *of* anything in particular. Just confident awareness. Just trust.

There is a story about a little monkey and the Buddha. The Buddha is sitting under a bodhi tree becoming enlightened after many, many lifetimes. After his awakening, waves and waves of doubt occur. Stones and demons hurl themselves at the Buddha. *Who says you are awake?* And the Buddha simply touches the earth to indicate 100 percent awareness, 100 percent absence of doubt about his being, 100 percent trust. *The earth is my witness.* As the Buddha's confidence and awareness expand and expand, a vast display of all the qualities of human goodness is spontaneously released—love, warmth, compassion, dignity, equanimity, kindness, intelligence, humor, wisdom. Nothing can make the Buddha turn back at this point, so he radiates a tremendous aura of authenticity, stability, and peace. A little monkey is watching the Buddha from a tree in the nearby forest, and the monkey is intrigued. "Hmmm. Look at what the Buddha's doing. Maybe I can do that, too!" So the little monkey takes its monkey mind, sits down on the ground, and imitates the Buddha's dignity.

As the Buddha's enlightenment continues to unfold, the little monkey relaxes more. In the process of sitting simply and being itself in a straightforward way, the little monkey starts to unravel its own monkey frivolousness. It rediscovers its own intrinsic qualities. Gradually, instead of trying to be the Buddha the monkey begins to warm up to being itself and being awake up in its own way. The little monkey begins to radiate little monkey wisdom and little monkey dignity. Now the situation around the monkey begins to evolve. The little monkey's friends become intrigued. "Hmmm. Look at what that monkey's doing. Maybe I can do that, too!" And they begin to uncover and proclaim their own basic goodness, confidence, and dignity.

What is it that the little monkey achieves? One hundred percent trust in itself. The absence of doubt. Self-existence. Openness that is definite and expanding. Confident awareness. Self-sufficiency. Strength. Discipline that evolves into realization. The monkey sat down and imitated the Buddha, and gradually the monkey overcame its doubts, just like the Buddha. It relaxed its doubts and fears, proclaimed confidence, and warmth and awareness radiated out.

The monkey's enlightenment, like the Buddha's, is not that its existence in the moment is almost completely workable, as if the monkey said, "I'm confident, you know, that is, if all goes well and things work out." Having 99.9999999 percent trust in your being isn't unconditional. If the Buddha or the monkey says, "That last corner of my being over there isn't covered by awareness, so there might be a problem in my being. I'd better not be fearless, because I don't know if that hidden corner in my being over there is completely trustworthy," then there's no victory, no well-being, no enlightenment, and no Buddha. *Buddha* means awake in Sanskrit. That last .0000001 percent of trust is necessary.

The story of the little monkey and the Buddha applies to ourselves. Every moment you come upon a fork in the road where you can give birth to yourself as a coward or as a brave person. One direction in the road has a sign that says, "Doubt yourself." If you take this road, you abandon being fully present. You don't trust being fully here. It's too open, too scary. Your nerves are too rattled. You're not confident. The other direction in the road has a sign that says, "As it is." On this road you *confirm* that there's no problem in your being anywhere. Your being is awareness, and awareness is expanding without stopping. That expansion is your discipline. Therefore you trust your basic existence 100 percent. This doesn't mean you don't communicate, go to work, have problems, and do what you do, but you trust unconditional awareness as your working basis.

You have something more than basic goodness in you. As a human being your heart can be challenged. Because you can be challenged, you have the possibility of fear, and therefore you also have the possibility of fearlessness. There is a fork in the road in every moment. Pushed by our habitual patterns, we make a choice very fast. Usually before we know it, we *find* ourselves cowardly, or we *find* ourselves brave; therefore, we express a warrior's courage by working with all the little doubts and fears in everyday moments in order to change our habitual patterning. Every moment, take down any barriers between yourself and your world. Every moment, refrain from doubts about your dignity.

This may seem too mundane for a warrior's discipline, but you are trying to organize the entire atmosphere around you into one that's brave and visionary. You are trying to do whatever you do in an open, doubtless, and fearless way. In this way every moment is the warrior's playground, and every moment counts. It doesn't mean you are a superhero. You are a human being. You can *doubtlessly* have doubt. You can *fearlessly* have fear. Practicing in this way, you can become a truly gentle and courageous human being. You open your heart when no one's looking, just again and again as you brush your teeth, take out the garbage, answer the phone, and do what you do. This may not seem like enough courage for everyday life because it's too small, and no one else will notice you are being brave. So what? This *is* courage in everyday life. It all begins here. Then when larger-scale situations happen, you can be seamlessly brave. You will know how to have a mind that's gentle and flexible, a mind that has vast possibilities of acting skillfully. The larger-scale situation won't be different than any other situation, and you'll find yourself being courageous. It truly works this way.

It isn't easy to achieve unconditional trust in ourselves. It isn't easy to refrain from needless doubts, fears, and second-guessing. Usually when we decide to refrain from something, we shrink our awareness instead of trusting our awareness and we tighten up our boundaries. "I'm addicted to popcorn. I'm going to renounce popcorn." Instead of being gentle we assert ourselves to make the rules clear. "From now on any popcorn that comes in with the groceries will be stored in the garage." We put up boundaries and alarm systems. "No more popcorn on the grocery list." We set up very tight boundaries. "No popcorn, no cigarettes, no more late-night movies, no anger, no more lust, no chocolate except on Sundays." But in Shambhala the warrior the dynamic is different. You rest in your nature as awareness. You relax instead of tightening up, so that anything that separates you from your experience, any wanting to be safe and comfortable, any doubt that you can handle things openly, victoriously, and in a completely dignified way is removed.

Years ago I saw a photograph of a Southeast Asian tapestry. The tapestry was intended as a representation of the Buddha's enlightenment. Instead of the usual image of a seated Buddha, cross-legged, radiating peace and equipoise, it was just the image of a begging bowl going upstream. No Buddha. No seated posture. No meditative equipoise. Just threads of a tapestry woven to indicate a current flowing downstream and the Buddha's begging bowl going upstream against the current. I thought, "That's *it*. That's why they call it practice!" We are going *against* the current of our habitual patterns. This takes a lot of gentleness, exertion, and encouraging ourselves.

In the example of the tapestry I think we are the begging bowl and also the stream, the shore, and the person who wove the tapestry. All the dimensions of meaning are personal. Whether you are going with the current or going upstream, you are going solo. If you base your courage on what others say, you might feel like you are going with the current for the moment, so now you're not really alone—"There's safety in numbers, so I'll be like the other people." But courage and confidence are more basic than that. In Shambhala the ultimate definition of courage is not being afraid of yourself, not doubting yourself, not cutting yourself off from the larger vision that's in you. Therefore every moment counts.

The discipline of courage in everyday life is to *cultivate what uplifts the situation and refrain from what degrades it*. What uplifts your situations is confident awareness, and what degrades your situations is any barrier that shuts your awareness down. Sometimes Rinpoche's students would sputter that this wasn't sufficient. We'd ask him, "*How* do we do this?" And he would say, "There's no how. You just do it. You just do." And, "I think you can do it. Just do it." *Just do it.* Any barrier between yourself and your world, any scheme, all those little thoughts and plans you have—you just take down the fences they are putting up. This is a discipline of exposure and nakedness because all you're left with are your awareness, your open heart, your strength, your nakedness. The whole thing adds up to making you more intelligent. Because you know what to cultivate and what to avoid, now you can improvise your behavior and insight without having to watch yourself unnecessarily, without having to "go by the book." There's no fixed plan for what you need to do, except to renounce not feeling things properly and not opening out. Then gradually the sun comes up.

"Sun" here means creativity, wisdom, unobstructed energy, greater intelligence. This doesn't mean your life will be without chaos, or the situation you are working with will have a positive outcome. In one way the chaos in your life increases because situations become more unpredictable, the more you let go of your fixed ideas of things. Yet equally your life becomes more predictable because a next step is always there for you. There is *always* a next step. It is built into your setup as a human being.

I heard a story on the radio about a UN doctor. Earlier he had worked to stop the ebola crisis in Africa, and now he was working with the AIDS crisis in Africa. At one point he was threatened by government officials who tried to shut down his clinic. The interviewer asked him, "Don't you get discouraged?" He said, "Well, my emotions do go up and down. When the helicopter with the soldiers came to get me, I refused. Yes, I was frightened. But no, I don't get discouraged." The helicopter that came to get him left without him and crashed on its way back to the capital city. "The whole thing showed me that life depends on nothing. It is very fragile. When I see what's happening, it makes me more determined to help."

There is a story about Avalokitesvara, a great warrior in the Buddhist tradition. In the story, Avalokitesvara dedicates himself to the benefit of others, and he saves all sentient beings—animals, humans, hell beings, ghosts, gods and goddesses, and so on. After he does this, he goes up to one of the heavens, called Tushita Heaven, where a Buddha dwells, and Avalokistesvara says, "I did it! I saved all sentient beings!" And the Buddha says, "That's really very wonderful! Good for you," and so on. Then the Buddha tells him to turn around and look behind him. Avalokitesvara turns around, looks, and sees an endless ocean behind him that's filled with sentient beings, each one of whom is suffering. Avalokistesvara's commitment is so great that at that moment his head splits into one hundred heads, his arms split into one thousand arms, and his fingers grow webs between them to save all the invisible beings, too. There is a famous Buddhist statue you may have seen of a bodhisattva (*bodhisattva* is Sanskrit for someone with an awakened heart) who has hundreds and hundreds of arms. This is Avalokitesvara, whose limbs represent limitless skillful activities inseparable from wisdom. If you trust yourself completely, if you are open to limitless skillfulness, then like Avalokitesvara and like the AIDS doctor in Africa seeing suffering, your determination grows stronger. Once compassionate vision is awakened, then your strength, longing, and inspiration increase in unexpected ways.

I think the difference between great warriors for humanity and you and me is not confidence in human goodness. It's not even that confidence comes easily to them, while you and I struggle day to day. It takes real manual work for anyone to strengthen their heart, especially when all around us there is war, poverty, plague, famine, degradation of the human spirit, and the threat of destruction of the planet. I think it's that their confidence is irreversible because they have so thoroughly connected to greater vision, so they work tirelessly for the benefit of others. They never, ever give up on human beings, whereas you and I watch the news, or are challenged, and have our doubts.

11

Discovering Greater Vision

·■· ·■· ·■·

Ground: Human beings are innately visionary.

Path: Cultivating openness, wakefulness, and
forward-looking discipline.

Fruition: We develop the capacity to listen to and
communicate our wisdom.

WHEN we say "vision," usually we mean a concrete picture
we have in our minds that serves as the North Star inside ourselves. *Vision* describes how you or I want to be, and how we
want people, the environment, leadership, our own qualities, our
society, and our relationships to be. It implies a set of values.
When I focus on vision, it empowers me by acting as a guide for
decision-making and relationships on a day-to-day basis. You
and I use vision as a foundation for action and for learning. We
constantly refer to it and never perfectly attain it.

Because we never perfectly attain vision, vision is never purely a concept. It is always an experience of longing. In Shambhala this longing is natural to human beings. Longing or being visionary is like an innate strength or strong orientation you have in you. Trungpa Rinpoche described it as an instinct you have toward reality rather than fantasy and as an aspiration to go beyond your own small world. There is a greater intention, a forward energy, an absence of depression, a brave aspect that's part of having a soft spot at all. In Shambhala there is an aspect of your soft spot that intrinsically says, "Ahhhh! This is my world. I am awake. So be it!" *before* it says, "Ooooh! Turn down the light. Make things small and snug. This is too bright!" Rinpoche said, "It's like an oomph in you. You've had it for a very, very long time, ever since human beings decided to go upright." As human beings you and I have a basic curiosity and forward-looking vision to see a larger world and contact reality beyond ourselves *before* we become afraid for our security and veer away. In this sense, there is nothing out of reach or out of the ordinary about being visionary. Purely because you are human, you have confidence to take a next step. The logic is that you *are* confident; therefore you can *choose* to be confident or not. In Buddhism and Shambhala you have greater vision because you can afford to have greater vision. Vision is based on your resources rather than on poverty or guilt.

For example, each time you come through a personal crisis, you have the opportunity to learn something about yourself. In this moment of learning, you can gain a vision that allows you to take the next step. Sometimes you can use what you have learned to help someone else. "I know for a fact that because there is a spark of health, inquisitiveness, and togetherness in me, it's in you, too. It may not flourish in you right away, and I don't know your experience, but I do know a spark of health and goodness is possible." Being visionary is like that.

There is a phenomenon called *teaching dreams* that aids in the development of confident vision. People call certain dreams "teaching dreams" because they teach you with unusual clarity what you need to know. Even if you're sleeping deeply, somehow teaching dreams get through. In one of these, I dreamt I was Superman. It was a beautiful, sunny, clear day, and I was flying in a clear blue sky in my blue Superman suit. The wind was in my face and I was looking down at Metropolis and enjoying the view, with my Superman cape flowing behind me. Then it occurred to me: "If I'm Superman, I must have a big S logo on my chest." So I looked down at my chest. The scene changed. Where the logo was supposed to be, there was nothing but an experience of my heart, which was huge and filled with love. When I woke up, I felt a little encouraged about myself. I think greater vision is part of our basic resources like that. "I have eyes, ears, the sun, the moon, sky, a brain, legs to walk with, the earth to sit on, a heart, and vision. I have a vision of human goodness."

Violence and cruelty around us are devastating because we have this instinct that tells us things could be different for human beings. We only notice that things are terrible or others are suffering because we have a basic vision of goodness. Even the most hardened person has this vision, although it may be buried very deep. The hard-hearted person may use a vision of human goodness as the North Star they want to destroy inside themselves and in their environment. Still, it's there. And it's because we see bleakness as well as promise around us that we need courage and dignity every day.

Vision is different than basic goodness because basic goodness isn't biased and vision is. Basic goodness pervades everything you perceive or could perceive and everything you experience or could experience—an orchid, a bomb, smelly trash, compassion, depression, pleasure, farming, skateboarding, cooking, birth, and death. Whether you are a great chef, a great lover, popular, shabby, frightened, young, old, lonely, in love, chubby, or skinny, you *are* basic goodness and you *have* basic goodness. Basic goodness is like the sun. It doesn't really care about you or not care about you. When the sun shines, it doesn't shine on some things and not on others. It couldn't care less. It just releases its rays and they go everywhere. There's no bias in the sun and there's no bias in basic goodness.

But vision is different. Vision is basic goodness biased toward humanity. You and I belong to a family of human beings. Everywhere you look you can see humans' vision of human goodness. Houses, farms, factories, schools, streets, electric lights, computers, tools, and art, utensils that you eat with, that buildings have doors near the ground so you can enter them, that forks have prongs to spear your food with, that cars have wheels to roll on— these are all expressions of greater vision. That you have four seasons and calendars, that traffic lights flash green for go and red for stop, that the directions north, south, east, and west make sense to you—all this is vision. At the moment you may not like the street or road you're walking on, but that there are such things as roads that lead from one place to another *at all* is an expression of one or more person's gentleness, realism, community, and courage. It is an expression of vision.

Wherever there are human beings, there is potential to bring out the goodness of humanity as an ultimate positiveness and solidity. Trungpa Rinpoche used the analogy of the *sun* to indicate the qualities of greatness, directness, and power in our nature. Throughout history cultures have used the analogy of the sun for this, too. In the analogy, the sun's *greatness* represents strength, energy, and power in you purely from being a human being. Earth has earth power, wind has wind power, fire has fire power, and human beings have human power, too.

If you look just below the surface of your everyday consciousness, in the very moment, despite your difficulties, there are no really *fundamental* problems anywhere. Maybe you've made a mess of things. You are a murderer. You hit your little brother when your mother wasn't looking. You lied to the press or to your boss. You cheated on a test. Now you're in jail or in the hospital. But still, life isn't purely two-dimensional, automatic, or mechanical. Even when you break society's rules, you are not an object or a thing. The analogy of the sun means that all human beings, purely by being human, can develop themselves. There is always the possibility of greater vision to go beyond our own small world and concepts. Sun means great, open, vast, the total absence of ignorance. You always have the potential to take a fresh look and make a fresh start. You have strength or greatness purely from being open by nature, from being and having basic goodness, regardless of how you use this potential in you.

The sun in this analogy also symbolizes *well-being*. You can relax into your nature as effortlessly as the sun releasing its rays. Fundamentally your energy is already fulfilled, therefore you can achieve your discipline, because a next step is always there for you. Purely from being a human being, a personal journey is under way, awareness is there to guide you, and you have what you need to work with what's in front of you. Warmth, engagement, and shining out are always possible. Purely from being human beings, we have creative energy and confidence.

A friend told me of a time he was lost in a neighborhood, so he went into a local bar to ask for directions. Everyone was so happy, positive, and chic that no one noticed him. He said, "I was invisible," so he radiated happiness and chicness and became one of them so he could be noticed and get the directions he needed. He said, "That's when I found out. Wow, the whole of reality is made up!" We create our reality every day. When you walk into a store, and the clerk says, "Can I help you?" it is an open situation. What you or I do the next moment creates reality. The simplest glance can affect things positively or negatively. In Shambhala the greater vision that is innately human radiates confidence, is peaceful, and has the potential to illuminate how to be a fully *human* being, a superhuman being. This vision is of human beings as powerful, wakeful, and relaxed; open, aspiring, and confident; disciplined and fulfilled—*naturally visionary*. When you look at vision in this way, it's simpleminded and also very potent. Once you discover you have this kind of instinct in you, you begin to cheer up immensely about yourself and others, too.

Sometimes the expression of vision in our actions is very small and close in. "Just get me through this day, this hour, this headache." Sometimes it's very big. "My people need a homeland where we can build a decent community." The Shambhala tradition says that human beings *fundamentally* look up, look out, and look ahead. Therefore you can be brave and expand, be brave and expand, be brave and expand. There is greater vision in you that is inspired about human possibilities. It is naturally open, peaceful, and confident. Regardless of our differences, this is what we share as human beings. It may feel like you need to turn inward first to find it, but greater vision is right there on the surface in you and in the atmosphere around you. You're just not seeing it until you soften to yourself. Then it manifests naturally.

Once you discover greater vision in you, the next step is to relax as you do what you do. Then the wisdom that's naturally in your body, speech, and mind has an opportunity to unfold. You have a chance to look good, speak well, and radiate a general sense of well-being and wholesomeness. The more you can project this, the more everyone feels better in your presence, including yourself. If you can do this, there's no extra thing you have to do to be a decent human being. You can be as you are, and that way you communicate what is positive about humanity.

12

Magical *Windhorse*

·■· ·■· ·■·

Ground: Windhorse is inherent life force or vitality.

Path: Increasing our connection to this universal energy.

Fruition: We are able to deal powerfully with
challenges and coincidence.

EACH one of us needs energy to fulfill our sense of vision. As we live our lives, we are constantly relating to the flow and exchange of energy. We gather in, concentrate, direct, use, smooth out, spend, rouse, relate to, replenish, communicate, celebrate, ignore, leak, and heal our energy. We say, "I had the energy to try something new, and the results were great." "The energy in the group is down." "I don't have the energy for this—my heart's not in it." "The energy shifted, and everybody clicked." "The energy on the conference call was cautious."

"When the detective entered the house, the energy didn't seem right." "The energy in the room shifted when I said that." "His energy is off."

We check on the energy between us. "Does my attitude convey the right amount of harmony or conflict?" "What energy am I sending in this message?" "What's the best way to organize and lead this team?" "What can we do to tap this team's creative energy?" "Who should be invited to dinner? What kind of energy do we want?" "We were able to accomplish more than we thought. Our energy was at an all-time high." We wonder how to increase the energy in our organization, at the dinner table, with our kids, and with ourselves. We wonder how to tap and increase creativity and energy.

Energy is a constant natural process in us and around us. Some scientists say that four percent of the universe is matter and the rest is energy. Still, in large part we don't pay attention to energy. When fear blocks our senses, our perceptions become numb. Our creativity is blocked. We can't read the environment and we can't read ourselves. We look for a hidden meaning to someone's action when it's all on the surface. We react to what's happening on the surface and miss the subtleties. Someone looks at us the wrong way and our energy goes down. Someone praises us and our energy goes up. We become drugged by our commentary, so we can't read what's actually happening. On the whole, we don't have a real command over energy.

Trungpa Rinpoche pointed out that the more you go into fear, the more you realize your fearlessness consists of real energy. This energy is not all-smiles, all-accepting, and all-accommodating. It is a power to shift, a power to accomplish, and a power to overcome. Rinpoche called it the *living aspect* of fearlessness and the only, only fuel for the journey human beings are on.

This living aspect of yourself, which is strong, speedy, and uplifted, is a life force that carries you beyond self-concern. It has a forceful, visionary quality, and it carries you outside the cocoon. In Shambhala, it is called *windhorse*. *Wind* is the energetic aspect of this life force—it is strength, power, and exuberance; and *horse* is your courage—how you individually capture, harness, and ride this powerful energy to overcome obstacles and accomplish what you intend. You may have obstacles of doubt, depression, hesitation, blockages in your senses—obstacles are anything that is in the way of you realizing the flowing and all-pervasive quality of basic goodness. Obstacles are what strong *windhorse* overcomes.

Windhorse is the energetic aspect of basic goodness, the flow of life, an alive, exuberant, and conquering energy that is always at your service, whether you are aware of it or not. The exuberant quality is the *wind*—direct and on the spot right away, a confident energy that is effortless, fearless, and accomplishing. *Horse* is the sustaining power because you can wield this energy like riding a horse or using the hilt of a sword to wield the blade. *Horse* is the discipline, stability, and majestic aspect because you can use this exuberance to ride the circumstances around you. It represents the unique application of exuberance to your own reality, to the warriorship you execute in your own individual situation. Combined, they become *windhorse*. You can use *windhorse* to ride coincidence with unique courage, power, and dignity.

Coincidence is the meeting together of situations or conditions. Incidents in life are constantly creating a particular unique situation, and if you are able to meet the present coincidence as it is, you can develop tremendously confident *windhorse* because you can see that what you do with the present coincidence as it relates to the future is completely up to you. The present is real as it is, and the future is a completely open one. Athletes experience this when they are playing "in the zone." Women giving birth experience this. Everyone at some point has had the experience of being completely and powerfully in the present with *windhorse* energy. Again, the *wind* aspect represents being present in an extremely direct way, and *horse* represents your unique chivalry and bravery. This energy is called a *magical windhorse* because it works. It affects things. It is a power to accomplish and a power to overcome any doubts you have. When you use it, you cheer up. Your body, speech, and mind are strengthened, and you are able to deal powerfully with your life.

Before I knew about Buddhism or Shambhala I was hiking with friends in the High Sierra mountains of California. The area we were in had a spacious, pristine, and rugged quality. One day some young men came to the mountain next to us and began throwing boulders into the crevasses, which disturbed us a lot. I stood up tall and hollered at them, "Hey! Cut it out." They looked at me like I was crazy because a huge deep crevasse at least two hundred yards across separated us. They kept rolling boulders over the cliff. I grew stronger. "I mean it! Cut it out!!" It was a strange moment. I felt I would fly across the crevasse and suc-ceed—I was that determined. They looked dumbfounded, then they stopped, drooped, and went away. I said to my friends, "I don't know what got into me." Now I'd say, *windhorse* got into me.

You can draw on *windhorse* to uplift yourself and change your state of mind, whatever your state of mind is, on the spot. You can gather it in whether you are on a subway, at work, in your garden, or at the beach. It is an endless bank of energy to which you are connected naturally, which has endless banks of resources, inspiration, and natural positiveness, and you can draw on it like drawing on a bank account. However, you don't have to go in, talk to the bank manager, fill out forms, and pay your money first. It exists as endless resources and endless wealth. Exuberant energy is at your service, all the time. It never runs out. Purely from being a human being, an endless uplifted energy is always there to draw on. A preexisting spark of confidence is there and you can pull it out of the blue, no matter your circumstances.

As human beings we take it for granted because it's basic to life. Different cultures call it different things, but it is the *human spirit,* our *spiritedness.* There is an unconditional longing, aspiration, or inspiration in you that is connected to having greater vision. It is a part of our human equipment that has inspired human beings for millennia. It stands on its own, like life force. Even in the worst of situations, as Anne Frank's diary shows us, a sense of vision and unconditional inspired energy can come through. It's not that some of us can access it and others can't. All humans are born with greater vision and *windhorse* energy. When you use them together, you are able to deal powerfully with your challenges.

Rinpoche said *invoking windhorse* is like raising a sail to catch and use a wind. The greater the energy you need, the greater your yearning or aspiration has to be, which is the sail, the greater the spirit or power you can capture, which is the wind, and the more powerful the circumstances you can ride. You can invoke a typhoon or a little breeze, depending on the kind of conquering and visionary power you need.

On an ultimate level, *windhorse* is unconditional vitality. Ultimately, it is an unconditional yearning to harness the formlessness or basic goodness in your being and use it to make a shift. When you rouse this ultimate yearning, the vitality that you are invoking literally comes to you. In the Shambhala tradition you do this purely to get out of the cocoon and celebrate life. You rouse a particular kind of energy in order to catch something preexisting, which is a powerful yearning to harness and ride basic goodness all the time, to fulfill your vision, and to shift any energy that exists toward positiveness and life. An energy, power, and spark exists in the space, and you put out your intention, your yearning, your good head and shoulders, and you catch the exuberant force, so that you uplift, energize, and empower yourself.

So—*windhorse* is what you rouse in yourself, and it is also the power that is being tapped; it is preexisting and inexhaustible vitality. You are using relative energy to capture ultimate energy to realize basic goodness, so you can increase your connection to your own life force and go beyond your cocoon. In Shambhala *windhorse* is vitality, a sense of gallantry, cheerfulness, uplifted-ness, and gentleness all bundled into the state of being a super-human being. It is the flow of life, the energy to accomplish, and the energy to overcome.

I think this isn't so out of reach. As a human being you relate to *windhorse* instinctively as you go about your day. You are always trying to overcome something in order to accomplish something. Warriors shout before going into battle. Team members shout before going out to play competitively. People build up their posture before singing, making a cold call, or having an interview. When you shift your energy to lift up your spirits because someone needs to talk to you, in that moment you are galvanizing the flow of life. You invoke an uplifted energy. When you open a window to refresh yourself, when you smile to lift up your spirits, in that moment you deliberately invoke uplifted energy. You pull energy out of the space to carry you beyond self-concern. You use it to heal wounded situations you are in. When you lift your head to look straight at the world, or put a spring into your step, or fix your tie in order to lift your spirits up, in that moment you invoke vitality and visionary energy. When you have good head and shoulders, this is due to *windhorse.* That you can sit in meditation and take a regal atti-tude to your life at all is due to *windhorse. Windhorse* shifts you to a larger view.

Takeda Shingen was a great warrior who lived in fourteenth-century Japan. He gave a very famous teaching to warriors under his leadership. He said they should develop their mind to be *fu rin ka zan*. One of my teachers, Kanjuro Shibata XX Sensei, translates these four syllables like this. FU: *Swift as the wind.* RIN: *Quiet, still, calm as a small grove of trees.* KA: *Direct, all-encompassing, complete as fire.* ZAN: *Immovable as a mountain.* This is a mind that has *windhorse* energy.

Once I asked Shibata Sensei, "What is the heart of a samurai?" He deflected my question with, "Samurai, samurai. I don't know about samurai heart. Samurai was two hundred fifty years ago. That was Japanese military samurai. But today there is no war. Everybody has the same life. Samurai today? I doubt it." "But, Sensei," I asked, "is the teaching of the great warrior Takeda Shingen also gone?" He said, "Trungpa Rinpoche always wanted to know about this. He asked me many times about this." I said, "Sensei, samurai heart is *something*. What *is* it?" He said, "It's difficult to discuss. It is unique to the person." But I wouldn't give up. "But, Sensei, is samurai heart that you never give up on yourself?" He said, "That's it! Never give up. Never, ever give up on yourself, or anyone!" This is greater vision and *windhorse* combined perfectly.

No one really, ever, finally can tell you what your unique courage should be because when you leave your cocoon, your courage is completely fresh, relevant, and up-to-date. To leave the cocoon you need strong *windhorse* so you're not subject to depression, habitual patterns, chaos, or someone else's power. *Windhorse* energy is something you have, and you have had it for a long time. You can invoke it, tap it, tune into it, and ride it. Everyone without exception is born with personal dignity, power, and energy. This has nothing to do with power over anything *in particular.* It is the energetic aspect of basic goodness. It is the living aspect of fearlessness, the life-force quality, in you.

Many traditions have ways to rouse and use this energy. Cultures use weapons, banners, flags, colors, and jewelry to capture *windhorse* energy. It can be captured in objects, the atmosphere of a room, a mustache, teacups, and tools. Groucho Marx captured and displayed it in his eyebrows and cigar. The military captures it in pins worn on the chest as well as in epaulets, certain weapons, and uniforms. A writer might capture *windhorse* energy in her pen or keyboard, which is her weapon. In Central Asia you can see flags decorated with a beautifully spirited horse. These are *windhorse* flags. They are placed on top of buildings, over doorway entrances, and at mountain passes to remind residents and travelers of a fantastically uplifted and conquering energy. The names warriors are given—Snow Dancer, Crazy Horse, Indestructible Mountain, Bad Hand—express how individuals are uniquely brave in catching and harnessing *windhorse,* how they uniquely proclaim the endless goodness, power, and accomplishment of human beings. In Shambhala it is when you can raise *windhorse* that you are known as a warrior.

The degree of skillfulness by which you harness *windhorse* is the degree of power that you have. Some people have tremendous *windhorse.* They display it as charisma, presence, a sense of radiance and command. There is no tentativeness in their being. You feel they have realized something. "That person has good *windhorse.*" Certain animals have good *windhorse.* They have the ability to rouse, concentrate, and ride their dignity.

Your dignity waxes and wanes depending on how you treat *windhorse.* Your spirit can be wounded through illness, accidents, aggression that comes at you, or aggression you put out. Your connection to *windhorse* can be harmed from too much loss, too much success, or having a wrong relationship to stress, alcohol, your friends, or anything. When you respect your clothes and treat them well, it strengthens your connection to *windhorse* because your clothes proclaim your relationship to the world. When you treat a captured enemy well, you acknowledge your own dignity and strengthen your *windhorse*. And your behavior can be *anti-windhorse,* too, which isn't a good idea. When you treat a captured enemy or a friend badly, it degrades and weakens your *windhorse*. When you say to yourself, "There goes a decent person and look at me—I can't move forward in the simplest way," this is *anti-windhorse*. When you lose your mind when you grapple with the garden hose, it takes its toll. On the whole when you treat your body, speech, mind, and world with disrespect, it's *anti-windhorse*.

What kind of *windhorse* you rouse to connect to your vision depends on what your obstacles are, how much reality is coming at you, and how skillful you need to be. It doesn't matter whether you invoke *windhorse* energy to get out of bed, walk your dog, run for president, or be kind to the person in front of you. The energy of fearlessness of great leaders you admire and the fearlessness executed by you is the same. It has the same nature. You're calling on the same force. You share the same humanity. You may have to invoke *windhorse* one hundred times throughout the day to remove the doubt that's holding you back from engaging with your world. That's all right. Each moment you rouse *windhorse* creates an impression on your heart.

Everything we've discussed leads up to this. Clear seeing allows you to look at things directly and realistically. And *windhorse* gives you the vision and energy you need to go forward. In Shambhala these two aspects, the warmth to appreciate things as they are and the fearlessness to engage, make up your nature. Together they constitute a powerful creative energy that you can use to command your world. It's up to you how much you use it and what you use it for.

With *windhorse*, life becomes more enjoyable because the more your heart is open, the more you understand life, the more you are able to realize the wisdom and beauty in things, and the more you are able to mold the world into patterns based on your appreciation and fearlessness. This is the accomplishing magic of *windhorse*. You are able to appreciate what is in front of you, situations and people, not see them as impossible, and work with whatever comes up.

You can use *windhorse* to take you to your meditation cushion. You can use *windhorse* to get up from your meditation cushion. Use it to activate your intelligence, to give you confidence to do what you need to do when you're having doubts. Use *windhorse* to strengthen your heart, mind, and body. Use it, use it, use it. *Windhorse* is unconditional, but you can't take its strength for granted. Every moment you need to check yourself. "Is what I'm doing, where I am, and what's happening strengthening *windhorse* or diminishing it?" In the tradition of Shambhala, it is always important to rouse *windhorse* because the cocoon is always challenging you.

13

Attaining Dignity

·■· ·■· ·■·

Ground: Accomplishments generate charisma or presence.
Path: By making our inner journey without doubt.
Fruition: We radiate an atmosphere of authenticity and dignity.

WHEN you rouse *windhorse*, you gain genuine dignity in a situation. You gain being in the situation with an awake mind and open heart. It creates a presence or field around you, which radiates authenticity. This is attaining dignity.

Everyone knows someone who has a powerful presence. It could be someone in the news, a particular person in history, or someone you see in a store or on the street. The person generates an energy and power around themselves. When you are in their vicinity, you feel it. A friend was buying a cup of coffee in a neighborhood shop in San Francisco, and the president of the United States came in and shook his hand. My friend said, "I didn't even vote for him, and I was bowled over! His energy was so powerful that I felt it all day!" A great Tibetan Buddhist teacher came to the United States to give a ceremony that communicates unconditional dignity in the Buddhist tradition. In New York City a motorcade of traffic police escorted him, and some of the police went on in to the ceremony and spontaneously asked for his blessings because the power in the atmosphere captured them. A friend's father, who didn't approve of his daughter's interest in Buddhism, said after the ceremony, "Wow, that fellow has charisma!" I went to a baseball stadium to honor Nelson Mandela's visit to North America. Although the stadium was huge, when he walked into the stadium everyone felt it. His presence was so full of genuine warmth, courage, and dignity that everyone spontaneously stood up.

An atmosphere can be generated around you purely based on your outer accomplishments. For example, you can gain charisma by being a powerful artist, a powerful executive, a powerful entertainer or athlete, or a powerful leader in government. When others are in your presence, they feel as if they were near a wood-burning stove. But another kind of atmosphere is generated purely from accomplishing an inner journey. Unlike a wood-burning stove that needs fuel to keep burning, this kind of charisma doesn't depend on external circumstances. It is self-generating. This is genuine or *inner dignity*. You attain it from having learned to abide in basic goodness for a long time. This presence is based on an inner authority instead of an outer authority. With inner dignity there's a sense that you aren't hiding in a cocoon in any way, that you are completely open to meeting the world with spontaneity and compassion.

I had an elderly friend, an artist, who fought in the International Brigade during the Spanish Civil War. When I first met him, he was living on a small pension and didn't have any family. He was old and had emphysema. The day he was taken to the hospital where he died, he was emaciated and looked like a bum. He hadn't been shaved for weeks and he was extremely weak. When I went toward his room to see him, two nurses stopped me in the hallway and said, "Who *is* this person? He seems like such a *distinguished* gentleman." He was hooked up to tubes and machinery, conscious, and couldn't speak. Yet it hurt your heart to be in the same room with him because there was so much upliftedness coming from him. There was no resentment in him whatsoever. The *windhorse* of awareness he was generating was almost palpable. You could see that he was working very hard to keep up with the changes that were happening to him as he was dying. You had to have good head and shoulders just to be in the room with him—even the doctor said this. When a friend told him I was there, my friend opened his eyes and beamed at me. It was like looking at the sun, close up, and feeling its heat.

According to Buddhism and Shambhala, warmth comes from egolessness, and egolessness comes from not centering on oneself. This friend gave me a glimpse of the incredible expansiveness, warmth, and flowing quality of egolessness. As he was dying, he was so at home in basic goodness that he could let situations come about naturally and work with whatever they presented, even work with his own dying—not work with it philosophically, spiritually, politically, religiously, or in any special way, but just completely on the basis of pragmatism and warmth, without ego, and without resentment of any kind.

When he was ill during the years before his death, I gave him a set of watercolor paints. He was visibly annoyed. He gathered himself together, although he was weak and confined to his bed, and puffed up his energy. "I am an oil painter. I don't do watercolors!" After he died, a friend of his approached me and said,

"He asked me to give this to you after he died." It is a beautiful, strong, and masculine watercolor painting. I matted it in yellow for the sun, and it's hanging in my kitchen.

For us to be like this man in his dying, we have to give in to there being no predetermined outcome to our activity. For ego, this is terrible news. It's devastating. It's asking too much. "What about *me* in the situation?" "What if something happens and I don't like it? What if something else happens, and things get worse?" But once you have achieved authenticity, you have achieved dignity. Dignity is settling into basic goodness, so the circumstances in your living and dying become immensely fluid and workable. It takes a lot of exertion to make a home in the formless aspect of what's happening, but the result is freedom to move about, humor, kindness. Now you can let situations evolve in their own way and work with what comes up because you're not looking for, or guarding against, anything that's missing that you don't see. Whatever you encounter is basic goodness, so you can incorporate it and use it.

This doesn't mean that the person who attains dignity doesn't care or doesn't care to be effective. The person with inner dignity cares immensely. You don't roll over and let the world eat you up. Just the opposite. Your presence contains power because you aren't depending on others' expectations for what to do. You have achieved a state of spontaneous compassion. It is spontaneous because you communicate without struggle according to your vision of endless human goodness. And it's compassionate because you accommodate everything as already awake—the awake quality just needs to come out more, and your vision is to bring it out. This can be intimidating for other people because they can feel the power in your vision. It awakens greater vision in them, too. I certainly was intimidated by Trungpa Rinpoche because his compassion was huge and, to me, unpredictable, so my ego went nuts by being surprised. But when ego meets compassion, something authentic can come through. As a friend said years after Chögyam Trungpa's death, "I miss being messed with," and I do, too.

Usually we go about dealing with situations differently than with compassion. We see them in terms of what we can gain or how we can be hurt. "Show me your cards, then I'll make a move. Tit for tat, okay?" We lose track of ourselves. Sometimes ordinary life can end up being freaky, where you don't know who is who, what is what, which is which, what you feel, and what's really happening. So you muddle through. "I don't handle that kind of a person very well, but I do okay with these people over here." But what are you muddling your way through *to*? And wouldn't it be better if you could relax more? Wouldn't it be great if you didn't struggle so much?

A person who has attained dignity can go down the street, eat an ice cream, have a conversation, and close a business deal much better than this because he or she is open to whatever occurs and works with everything as another expression of basic goodness. When you attain dignity, you have worn out longing for another world. There is humor and power in your presence because you have so thoroughly related to yourself and gone beyond resentment. So your actions are accomplished gracefully and have purpose. This doesn't mean you levitate instead of having to take a taxi or the bus. It's not that the dignified person never cries. You don't have a life of pleasure and no pain. It's that your heart is open and your actions have compassion and accomplishment, so your body, speech, and mind manifest as dignity.

This is difficult for us. We think something bad is going to happen if we relax. We think there is some hidden agenda that can threaten us in the environment and in ourselves. We don't take invoking *windhorse* and attaining dignity seriously. "It sounds good, but you know, I don't have time, and I have my doubts."

Once I met a teenager who had been autistic since he was a child. When he was little, he'd been put in a terminal-care facility where they feed you and give you shelter, but don't provide conversation or talk therapy. After he had been there for years, he began to talk, which no one expected. This teenager told the doctors that he could get better. They said, "No, you can't." He said, "Yes, I can." They said, "No, you won't be able to. You're autistic." And he said, "I *can* get better. I *know* I can do it." So the doctors sent him to another hospital that conducted research on young people. He was strange. Whenever he felt awkward, he would stretch his head up toward the ceiling, call out, "Coo, coo," and talk about "the lambs." The lambs lived in a land above the aggression of everyday life. He had done this for years, and it had stretched his neck until it was really long, purely from longing for peace.

At a talent show put on by the patients, this shy young man gave an imitation of an ad for Benson & Hedges extra-long (one hundred centimeters) cigarettes. He got up on the makeshift stage, pursed his lips in front of the parents and doctors in white coats, and cooed, "Ooooooh the advaaaantages of the neeeew Benson & Hedges 100s." I thought it would break my heart. Was this a glimpse of an awakened heart? It doesn't matter if his genuineness wasn't stable, or whether he, I, the parents, nurses, or doctors could fully appreciate his accomplishment. He took his longing, his extra-long neck and awkwardness, the bizarre situation everyone was in, and bundled the whole thing up into joy and sadness. He gave us a glimpse of his beautifully genuine dignity.

In various traditions and cultures young people are given names during a rite of passage, and the name suits them. How is this possible? It's because they are appreciated. They display their own sense of greater vision, not vision as a specific objective, but their unique flair when they are at home in basic goodness. This is seen by the elders, and the elders give them their true name. Then in the ceremony these young people are also given a *wind-horse-rousing* practice to remove any doubts and misunderstandings they may have about being genuine because the elders want them to *be themselves at all costs.* This name stays with you your whole lifetime. "Hey, Harmony Morning, over here! Incredible Peony, Golden Poem, come here and help!" The point of the name is that it's you. It's your *windhorse*, and *windhorse* is your courage and flair. The community wants you to be the essence of what you are, be brave about that, and expand as you are. Then as you mature the elders grow you as an oak tree from an acorn, instead of an elm from a peanut or a horse from a tree. In this way the community is healthy, its wisdom is continuous, and you can succeed. If I could give the boy in the hospital one of these names, I would call him Flawless Dignity.

Recently there was a ceremony in India where one thousand people converted to Buddhism. They were "untouchable" human beings, which indicates the lowest of the low in Indian society. Traditionally, even the shadow of an untouchable person can't touch the shadow of a person from the Hindu upper castes. One of the people was interviewed on the radio. He said, "No longer am I untouchable. Now I am a liberated human being." He used this ceremony to proclaim his dignity.

In Shambhala dignity is a strength and style of courage and gentleness you use to engage with the world. It exists as part of your human nature, although it may be buried or manifest in a haphazard way. Once Rinpoche cried with tears, "Even cats and dogs have dignity. Why can't human beings, too?" When you lose track of the essence of yourself, individual courage becomes an issue. Somehow you forget yourself and you become confused. Then you must rouse *windhorse* to contact the energy of basic goodness and attain the dignity that is your inheritance.

14

How to Invoke *Windhorse*

·❚· ·❚· ·❚·

Ground: Windhorse generates a sense of life.

Path: By deliberately increasing its energy.

Fruition: We empower our purpose and our vision.

THERE is no point in talking about courage when you are on top of the world. Everyone has courage when they have a good state of mind. It's when the body is weak, your ability to relate with your situation is failing you, and the mind goes down that courage is important. When body, heart, or mind go down, in Buddhism and Shambhala all the methods come down to courage. All the instructions try to help you invoke a connection to life. Whatever the method is called, you are invoking *windhorse* energy.

In Shambhala invoking *windhorse* is a deliberate practice you can use to increase the energy that generates your sense of life. In this way it is a practice to uncover unconditioned confidence in yourself, display it, and awaken authenticity in your being. It's important to receive personal instruction in both mindfulness-awareness meditation practice and invoking *windhorse,* if you can. At the same time, these practices simply highlight natural processes that are already in you. They tap a state of mind that is open that you cannot fake. Both mindfulness-awareness and invoking *windhorse* acknowledge and use this. You can deliberately train to recognize, rest in, and use this awakened energy. Invoking *windhorse* does this in the following way, which I am presenting as a five-step process.

First, come into the present, which is always available. Take your seat. This is a metaphorical seat. It means to establish yourself where you are as you are. *This* situation is challenging, *this* mind is going down, *this* heart needs encouragement, *this* courage and dignity need more strength. Taking your seat is like clearing the ground for where your fearlessness will be executed. You are claiming *this* time and space and establishing your presence *here*. Bring simplicity to your body and mind. Feel the environment. You can say to yourself, "This is a good time and space to consolidate my energy. This is a good time and space to go forward. It is the time and space I have." It doesn't matter where you are. You may be sitting at home, washing the dishes, about to speak to your boss, or walking across a stage. You may be dying in a hospital bed. You are about to invoke energy, so you adopt a good *inner posture*. This brings respect and composure to your body and mind. No one can give this to you. It's contrary to human nature. You have inner good posture in you, and *you* have to adopt it. This comes with accepting the time and space you have and accepting greater vision. "This is a good time and place to execute bravery. It is good, because it is the time and place I have." Just taking this first step is meaningful.

Once you have adopted your inner good posture, now you have it. This is the second step. It sounds simpleminded. It is, and it's powerful. You are as you are, so now you can *confirm* your genuineness. Just feel yourself there. Everything is in its place. There is a sense of open space around you. The earth is supporting you. Everything is working as it should be. Everything is complete. You are here, with a vision and longing for yourself as brave and conquering. You would like to realize your greater vision. As you appreciate and confirm this yearning and intention, your inner space begins to change. It is as if you were declaring there is a forward to the space, which is straight ahead where your challenge is. Because there is a forward, the rest of the space begins to make more sense. Your relationship to your situation is changing and the atmosphere around you starts to transform, too. You are developing your genuineness and bravery.

The third step is to tune in to your awareness. This is abrupt. Just tune in. Bring your body and mind together on the spot. Empower yourself in this moment. Just plant awareness firmly in your body and mind.

Now you can relax more. Underlying everything is your gentleness and genuineness, and you can relax into that. In this fourth step, you are contacting your heart. Your heart is your confidence and strength, and you've found it. To feel your heart is joyful, strengthening, and slightly sad. You actually feel the confidence and genuineness in you as an experience of warmth, and the environment around you warms up, too. Your body and mind begin to fill with warmth the way a porous paper saturates with ink when you touch it with an ink-filled brush. This warmth is fearless, based on gentleness and realism. You are not stuck. This doesn't mean you will succeed with the challenge in front of you.

But it gives you the heartfelt energy you need, and therefore you are succeeding in being powerful as you are. *Windhorse energy* is spreading in your body and mind.

Finally, radiate out confident awareness in all directions. In this fifth step, just radiate as you are. You are still in your hospital bed, washing the dishes, walking across a stage, or about to speak to your boss. The difference is that you have found your confidence, so you can radiate out confidence in your body and mind. And you do. You have gained being present in an authentic way. You have gained the vitality and inspiration you need. Your senses are open. There is a sense of strength and life force in your body. Now you can continue with a new attitude and new energy. Make your phone call. Speak to your boss. Address what's intimidating you. As you continue with your situation, you can come back to this sense of greater strength and life force in you again and again. You've connected to *windhorse* energy, and now the wisdom in you and the wisdom in the situation aren't separate. This is conquering and enjoyable. Having raised *windhorse*, you can work with what's in front of you simply and directly. Your vision is bigger than your obstacles.

Rousing *windhorse* as a formal practice belongs to the Shambhala tradition. I have finger-painted it at best, and it's a little odd for me to say to you, "Step one, step two," because the natural process of *windhorse* happens organically. Still, a formal practice seems necessary to bring out and highlight what we already do because we forget. If you don't take the process too solemnly, then the magic comes.

You can invoke *windhorse* slowly or invoke it in a flash. Study it. Find out more about it. Receive personal instruction. Invoke *windhorse* energy in your office, walking down the street, and at the mall. Rouse it when you're standing in your kitchen, approaching the speaker's podium, waiting for your appointment, or lying in bed. Go to a phone booth and, instead of telephoning, use the moment to turn your energy toward basic goodness and rouse *windhorse* energy. When you can't sleep at night, rouse your windhorse and see where it takes you. When you wake up in the morning, rouse your *windhorse*. Rousing *windhorse* is an inner process. You can do it anywhere.

You can write slogans and put them in your purse, on your refrigerator, and on the steering wheel of your car. When de Klerk received the Nobel Peace Prize along with Nelson Mandela, he said, "I don't claim to have succeeded, but what I set out to do, I did." I kept this as a slogan on my computer for years. If perseverance is what you need, this slogan has *windhorse,* and maybe it will help. Today a card on my computer says, "The warrior is supposed to be intelligent and listen to her heart. This is what my heart is telling me, so I'm telling you." Sakyong Mipham Rinpoche said this first. Just reading the words can increase your *windhorse* energy.

The energies of life are very powerful, and you are always at their center. How big your world is depends on how much you are able to open and how much reality you can handle. A friend wrote in an e-mail, "I used to be rather gallant about dying. Now it's just day-to-day. It's touch and go." When she died, I was given her favorite pin, which has on it a symbol of *windhorse* energy. She knew that *windhorse* was not about being 100 percent on top of things. It is not power over a situation, power over a circumstance, or power over anything except our own doubt. When you have strong *windhorse,* you are able to ride whatever comes up. Having strong *windhorse* doesn't guarantee that your actions will accomplish a particular outcome in the world. It won't save you from dying. The real result is your own courage and dignity. *Windhorse* unites your vision directly and powerfully with what's in front of you. This is why it is called *magical windhorse—*

because you overcome any sense of hesitation and fully empower yourself as you are.

In order to lead a meaningful life, you don't have to be consistent, create a coherent personality, or have a logic for yourself. You can just take advantage of basic goodness in you and around you as you live your life and do what you do. You don't need to live your whole life heroically without doubt! You just have to pop that thing that's in the way *now*. Just cheer up, remove your doubt about yourself, and move forward *now*. This is the function of rousing *windhorse* energy.

Life isn't a job where you wake up in the morning with a lid on your head, go to sleep at night with a lid on your head, and in between keep your nose clean (or dirty, depending on your view), get old, get sick, and die with a lid on your head. *Windhorse* is the vehicle to bring you out of the cocoon and put you in touch with the real energies of the world. When you capture it, harness it, and ride it, you achieve a state of being that is fulfilled. It doesn't wane. So along with the gradual developmental process of letting go of fixations and doubts about yourself, the practice of *windhorse* accomplishes this instantaneously, pragmatically, and beautifully.

On the whole, it takes a lot of vividness and radiance to see the basic goodness of ourselves and others. It takes activity on our part to have command of the coincidences that occur in our lives. In the tradition of Shambhala, it takes *magical windhorse* energy.

PART FOUR

The World as Friend

·■·

15

The World as Friend

▪ ▪ ▪

Ground: The world functions as a teacher.

Path: By opening further and extending ourselves.

Fruition: We discover our entire life is workable and a friend.

ONE summer I did a solitary retreat in the mountains of southern Colorado. The hut didn't have running water or electricity. The setting was isolated and beautiful, with caretakers I could reach by foot less than a mile away. The cabin was small and sweet. There was a woodburning stove in one corner and a bed built into the wall along one side. On the outside of that wall there was a propane tank that provided fuel for a cooking stove.

One evening I finished a meditation session, got into bed, and went to sleep. During the night a severe electrical storm came up over the Rockies. I woke up to tremendous explosions around the hut. The air was pitch black, then sliced with explosions of sound and light, followed by complete darkness again. Initially I had a few thoughts—"I can't run away because I can't go outside." "There is a lot of metal around me." "A full propane tank is inches away from where I'm lying." Then gradually I was left with no thoughts or fears because what was happening was so persuasive. It was utterly real, and there was nothing I could do about it. So it poured explosions and rain, and I lay there. "Bam! Bam!" I remember being extremely clear that my fear and thoughts were *not relevant*. Reality was functioning completely and very beautifully without me. The elements of earth, water, fire, and air were alive and interacting, and there was nothing I could manipulate anywhere.

At some point I blanked out. When I came to myself again, it was morning. I found Sheetrock all over my bed. The lightning had split a beam in the roof, and its force popped out a wallboard. I dusted myself off and went outside. The air was crystal clear, and the ground, stones, and trees were drenched. There was silence everywhere. My mind was absolutely quiet, washed clear of concepts that I usually use to separate things. A pack of coyotes came by, whimpering, lost and disoriented by the storm. Soon after that a few birds began to sing tentatively and then more strongly. Gradually a familiar and more habitual world was put back together again.

As I go about my day in the city, sometimes contacting the natural power in the world seems out of reach. But it's possible at any moment. This retreat showed me that. We just don't have confidence. The world functions beautifully and powerfully, in nature and on city streets, beyond the limits of our hopes and fears. As my thoughts and fears stopped during this storm, I realized the world wasn't an adversary. Reality was functioning flawlessly, and the trees, the rain, the sky, the earth, the animals, and I were sharing that reality flawlessly and effortlessly. Shocked out of my patterns, I wove myself into the world's natural functioning. I imagine that the coyotes, birds, and insects did this, too. As I reflect on how habitual patterns can shape and reshape, come and go, so unexpectedly, I think, "This very moment, too, is flawless, and part of natural functioning. When I am caught in fixed beliefs, I'm just not seeing clearly in my everyday life."

In nowness you are meeting *sacred world*. Every situation, without exception, is a real situation. Nothing is a rehearsal. Every situation can teach you something. The basic meaning of sacred world is that the world around you and the energies in you have natural potential to wake you up. *Sacred* doesn't mean that something is rare, precious, and always good, and that everything else is common, replaceable, and a throwaway. There is a living quality in the phenomenal world and in yourself that is unconditioned, not created. This living quality is an energy of friendship and nonaggression that manifests when you use acceptance and appreciation to weave yourself into its natural functioning. Nonaggression means it has its own power, beyond struggle of any kind.

The Shambhala teachings on the natural world are very powerful. They teach how you can be guided by and be elegant and commanding like the elements. These teachings merit their own treatment, but the point I'd like to make is this. You don't have to be walking in a quiet meadow to meet the natural world. You can meet the quality of natural nonaggression, sacredness, or friendship in your apartment, on New York City streets, or in a war-zone marketplace. You can meet it in your own body. Once on National Public Radio I heard music composed by a young man with the AIDS virus. He had used a synthesizer to record and play back the music of his own T-cells dying. It was very beautiful and haunting to hear his T-cells swoon and pass away. Finally, at the end of his composition, there was just space. I think this expressed beautifully meeting the world as friend.

Realizing the world functions without aggression, that it naturally functions as a friend to support and teach us, is such an immediate and direct experience that we are either encouraged by this, open up, and learn, or we tend to try to cocoon ourselves and move away a little bit. When we move away, things tend to get complicated and the sense of friendship is filtered out of our experience. For example, you go to a new grocery store, and the lettuce is in the wrong place, or it's wilted, or too wet. You feel challenged and resent the storekeeper. I lived in Toronto where there were huge postal boxes with teeny, weeny little signs that say "post." The postal boxes themselves were a dull camouflage color and hard to notice. It rattled me. I would wonder, "Where's the postal box?" Then when I'd find one I would wonder, "Is this really the letter box? Does it have a different purpose I don't know about?" I was lonely, adjusting to a new country, and looking for a mailbox put me over the edge. I told a friend, who said, "Well, it can't be that foreign. Pull yourself together. It's only Canada, for Pete's sake." One little obstacle to my habitual thinking, and my world went out of joint. In a moment like that we struggle to perceive, struggle to understand, and struggle to connect. Then imagine when something dramatic and serious like a war happens, or we are dying. I think, "If I can't handle a new mailbox or stubbing my toe, how am I supposed to handle this?"

In Shambhala the sacred world is always there. When you relax thoroughly, you see it. Even in something as simple as stubbing your toe, the world is trying to reach you and teach you. According to the teachings the world has been trying to do this for a very long time. It's always trying to do this. In this way the world is a powerful friend.

On the way to Shambhala Mountain Center there is a fork where a road turns off into the mountains of northern Colorado while the highway goes on to Wyoming. When you make the turn, you think, "The sky here is Colorado sky and ten miles north it is Wyoming sky, so I'd better turn here." But this isn't true. The sky has no boundaries. It is all one sky. It is our mind that fragments things. We divide up everything into humans, animals, my world, your world, the world of people like myself, the world of people who are different, the sky over Mexico City, the sky over me, men, women, different economic classes, different governments, your side, my side, you and me, us and them. The divisions are supposed to help you understand and engage, but instead they produce bewilderment, the bewilderment produces fear, and things begin to play off each other in aggression and conflict. When you try to conquer your fear, it uncovers your bewilderment. When you try to conquer your bewilderment, it uncovers your fear. It's like the morning after you've been at a loud and boisterous party. You think, "What happened at the party? Should I have been more outgoing, or should I call and apologize?" This is like the joke of who's on first and what's on second. Things play off each other as you struggle to understand a divided world. You make things complicated. You're caught in your thoughts, and now you think the world is unfriendly, so it can't reach you and teach you anything.

Meanwhile, the real world continues to do what it does—function naturally to counsel, guide, and, potentially, cheer you up. One spring a Mongolian dust cloud was moving over the western United States. It moved right over the city where I lived, and the newscasters showed the cloud on television. The weather forecasters laughed about how they had missed the class on Mongolian dust when they were studying to be meteorologists. But I sat there thinking it's astonishing how connected we are. I thought,

"A Mongolian dust cloud! It's a magical world." We are all one system. The friendship is that we always have endless possibilities to wake up, even in noticing a dust cloud floating by. All that's required is that *we* open up.

Being in touch with reality takes courage and strength. When the world becomes a waking-up principle, everything has a thought-provoking quality, a purpose of some kind, which makes you think twice or, as Trungpa Rinpoche said, think thrice about reality. Just living life can be like sitting down to a feast where the courses never end. You think, "Thank you, that's enough, I've learned enough today. It was delicious, and now I don't want any more!" but more courses, wines, and desserts are being delivered all the time. On top of that servants, musicians, dancers, and new guests you don't know start to arrive. The more you open, the more the world invites you to step out, and the more the feast of life goes out of your control. It takes strength to generate the power and radiance to stay open, so that instead of retreating to your habitual patterns you say, "Okay, let's go. The joke's on me!"

In the Shambhala teachings our world has brilliance and genuineness far beyond what our minds can grasp, and instead of withdrawing from it we are training to give in, give out, and appreciate. This is not based on trying to get a good or bad result. Instead, you realize you are in *continual* relationship with the world, and your world *will* give you a message. The theme is continuity, nonstruggle, nondivision, unification, friendship with the world. Victory occurs whether you have a success or failure, and you learn to be without aggression or confusion, to be in peace.

I have a friend who says he fell in love with me while watching me carve a fish. It's a good line and very funny, but I knew what he meant. I remember that the occasion was enjoyable and accomplishing—I appreciated the fish, the knife, the cutting board, the market the fish came from, the life it had lived, the ocean, the guests, the recipe, the meal being prepared, the whole thing. It wasn't self-conscious. When you experience an atmosphere of nowness and appreciation like that, it has a brilliance and flowing quality. It has an energy that is nonaggressive, that unifies.

You might experience something like this when you are enjoying washing your car. You appreciate the car and sponge, the weather, the water's spray that hits you, the dents, the gleam and grit, the workers who made the car, mechanics who have worked on it, gravel in your driveway, sunshine, that someone invented cars at all, your skill, the goodness of your body and mind. There is a kind of magic present, because there is no fundamental division between you and your world. The atmosphere is peaceful and accomplishing. There is relationship, flow, and the unification of *this* and *that*—the car, the dents, the water's spray, your body and mind, the factory the car came from, who's going to ride in the car, and the relationship of all those to one another—everything is relationship and appreciation. You are tuning in to how to wash a car, how to live life, and how to do anything. It doesn't matter that the experience is brief. It is teaching you something. You experience an alive and strong unifying energy that's so genuine that everything genuine, unified, and without deception *in yourself* is nurtured and increased. I am analyzing it, but in reality you just enjoy the sense of peace and accomplishment. You say, "I enjoyed washing the car. It was a perfect day to do this. I feel renewed. It gave me energy!" This unifying energy is always there, but *we* have to relax to connect to it. Whether we meet it or not depends on *how* we wash our car or do anything we do. When our activity has a broad and deep sense of nondivision, it has wisdom and power in it. There is no separation between our wisdom and the wisdom in the situation.

We remember times like these and draw energy from them. We use these experiences to celebrate life.

There is always some nonaggressive energy or quality in situations, which is available to teach and heal you and be friendly in this way. The way to contact it is to rouse *windhorse* and create an atmosphere of bravery around yourself. Bravery here means more than being beyond fear. It is active confidence. Your absence of doubt brings out a brilliance and genuineness in yourself and your environment, no matter what you are doing. Even in the worst circumstances you can be sustained because the world is naturally alive with this energy. Even when you feel you have nothing left at all, an unconditional nonaggression is there that you can contact and use.

This is the notion of *egolessness* in both Shambhala and Buddhism. Here egolessness means openness, appreciation, gentleness, and going beyond self-concern, so that anxiety and a sense of division disappear. The atmosphere brightens with a pacifying and unifying energy. On the whole, the less you act from ego, the more the world is your friend. The less ego, the more realistic you can be. The less ego, the more elegant you are because you let the world care for you, coach you, and wake you up. Even when you are dying, there can be an atmosphere of victory in the sense of peace and accomplishment, and the people around you feel it. When we are around this kind of energy, we feel uplifted and awake. We search for it all our lives, and all the time it is there in our world. It's up to *us* to generate an atmosphere of bravery and opening up. In this way every moment is always *the* occasion to open up.

An economist told a story about walking with his daughter in the woods. She said to her father, "There are monsters in these woods!" He said, "Okay, should we get guns?" She said, "Oh no, we should feed them!" The world isn't a dead world. The flow of life is powerful, and at any moment you can strengthen your relationship to it or be afraid of its power. This father offered his little girl a choice, and she chose to strengthen her relationship to the world, to celebrate its power and not be afraid. When you can acknowledge and celebrate your connection to life in this way, the result is an alive and flowing connection with your world.

A friend was having lunch in a minipark in San Francisco. There were two winos sleeping on park benches, very close to where he sat. As he told this story, he said, "When I work, I'm pretty disheveled, so when I sat down, I didn't look too much different than they did." The winos were sleeping and he began to have a ferocious conversation in his head with the winos. "They can get their act together!" "Don't they dare ask me for a nickel!" The winos were sleeping, and he was sitting on another bench, having this incredible conversation with them in his head. "Then," he said, "one of the guys just opened his eyes, gave me a beautiful smile, waved, and closed his eyes again. That was a wise man in those clothes. Who knows what was going on in his head, but it worked! This guy really shook me up."

Like the wino on the park bench who waves at you, the world functions as a teacher when you open up beyond your concepts. As you begin to appreciate this, everything begins to make sense. The world has always been there for you, teaching you what you need to know. Your whole life is workable and a friend, and you can use it. Bravery is part of your basic nature. Ultimately, this principle in you is always victorious—you can always access fundamental wisdom that harmonizes your world. You can always use the space and time you have. As a warrior you can keep a certain atmosphere around you all the time, based on your own courage and vision. That way you will have enjoyment and celebration because you are learning and being nourished by an atmosphere of spontaneous wisdom, skill, and elegance. You are using your mind, heart, and everything around you to wake yourself up.

16

Four Dignities

·■· ·■· ·■·

Ground: We use different styles of engaging our world.

Path: By being dignified in meek, perky, outrageous,
and inscrutable ways.

Fruition: We attain the pinnacle of being a fully human being.

ONCE you decide to wake yourself up, once you rouse *wind-horse* and contact the energy of basic goodness, everywhere you look you find an invitation to relax and appreciate the world. The more you accept the invitation, the more your confidence expands. In the Shambhala teachings this manifests as *meek, perky, outrageous,* and *inscrutable dignity.* According to Trungpa Rinpoche, these are four different styles we have of engaging with the world around us. Each dignity gradually develops into the next dignity as you open further to the world, so dignity is both an unfolding process and a discipline to learn. At the same time, when you are fully confident in the world, these four styles are fully available to use because dignity is part of your natural potential, whether it manifests brilliantly, haphazardly, chaotically, or not at all.

Meek Dignity

THE first style of engaging the world is *meek dignity*. Even just being curious about yourself, just looking at your energy and seeing its dynamic, is the beginning of dignity. Meek dignity means you open up, accept, and appreciate what you have. The opposite attitude is, "Ho hum, nothing to interest me here. One hundred percent familiar. I'm snug. Nothing can touch me about this." Instead, with meek dignity you appreciate even the smallest details. Therefore you stay eventempered in diverse situations, keeping your relationships with the world simple and fair. For example, if you work with many different people, because you appreciate the myriad details and innuendos in each relationship, you adjust yourself depending on whom you're dealing with— what you say, how you say it, what you emphasize, which part of you is brought to the foreground, what you send to the background. You bring something slightly different to each conversation and encounter. You still have opinions about things. You still have good and bad connections with others. But on a very basic level you've taken like and dislike out of the equation, so you have a very strong sense that you are genuine, that the world around you is always getting the real you. It's just that not everyone sees exactly the same side of you. In that way your style of engaging is skillful because you're being decent, friendly, flexible, and appreciative to what's there. Your decency comes from practicing friendliness to yourself, which brings appreciation and equanimity, and practicing mercy to the other, which takes away any arrogance or barriers. Others find you approachable because you provide a ground of fairness, which gives people ground for opening up. The more *they* open to you, the more *you* open because it further ignites your humbleness and inquisitiveness to the world, and this further increases your meek dignity.

A friend who was caught in a rolling chain of corporate lay-offs worked in a cubicle without any privacy. Her stress had been building for weeks. She felt she was next to be laid off, and she was trying to hold her poise and float with what was happening. One day she panicked, went to find someone to talk to, and passed by the president's office. He happened to look up. Later she said, "I don't remember how it happened. He smiled, and I felt a sense of invitation, so I went in." She sat down in front of him, put her head on his desk, and sobbed. "I guess he didn't know what to do, so he just listened! I sobbed and sobbed!" He didn't have arrogance, and he didn't try to put up barriers. Nothing like, "She's not me. I'm not her. Let her drown. Let her call Human Resources. I'm in the life raft." He said afterward that he felt sympathy; he knew more employees were being laid off, maybe himself included. She said that she had always felt a sense of security and stability when he was around, but that had been from a distance. Now there she was sobbing with her head on his desk! We laughed and cried when she talked about it. I thought it was an example, on both their parts, of meek dignity. Nothing was complicated by a lack of equality, and so these two meek warriors were both appreciative and approachable.

When asked about the number of people she had helped, Mother Teresa said, "I never counted. I just took one, one, one, one, one." Mother Teresa's response is another example of meek dignity. Meek dignity is percolating all the time. Without it operating in the background, you wouldn't be able to breathe, make love, sleep, eat your lunch, or argue about politics. There would be no flow to life, no exchange. Meek dignity is natural in this way. And when you attain it, you settle into appreciation. You have learned to rest in the simplicity of being a decent human being.

This is a big achievement. It may not sound like meek dignity is tough enough for this world, but how *is* it that people we admire have accomplished being approachable, skillful in varied situations, and fair? What is *their* inner state of mind that allows them to be respectful of their own experience and merciful to ours? It's not that they are timid. They are at home with themselves and they are at home with the world. In Shambhala *the symbol for meek dignity* is a tiger walking through the jungle. A tiger walking through the jungle is mindful, casual, confident, and powerful. Its dignity is carefree. It has so much dignity, there's no need for arrogance. When you are meek in this way, you are not complicated. You are simple, open, and without arrogance. Not needing approval, you are approachable. You are a genuine and basic human being, and so you present yourself that way, too.

Perky Dignity

ONCE you attain meek dignity, a further dignity unfolds like a flower that's blossoming. This is *perky dignity*. Here, your confidence is increasing, and your skillfulness is, too. The monumental knowledge and wisdom around you aren't seen as separate from you anymore. You are still appreciative of what's around you, but now you tune in further to your own wisdom. Your dignity has increased to become more carefree and confident. You manifest spontaneous know-how about how the whole world works.

You just jump to conclusions. You don't know where this wisdom comes from. You just find it. You just pull it out of the blue. It's in the situation, and you just say it. You just do it. You share your wisdom without hesitation. You just release your energy—which is a perky and cheerful thing to do.

My first date as a young girl was to a dance. I was thirteen, I had a crush on my date, and I was very excited. Before the dance my mother took me shopping. I bought a short-sleeved, soft, and fuzzy white sweater with a scooped neck and little white pearls sewn around the neckline. We also bought a black felt skirt with white felt English street lampposts sewn around the lower edge. When I tried it on, I thought, "Tasteful, sexy, and also pure"—I felt like I was becoming a woman. Also, in the white felt lampposts on the skirt there were tiny little lightbulbs like the kind you put on Christmas trees. The skirt was wired, and in the pocket of the skirt was a battery that I could plug into a switch. When I plugged it in, the little lights in the lampposts flashed on and off.

At the dance the lights in the hall were a little low, and I'm sure the chaperones thought it was sweet to see their kids slow-dancing. My date seemed to like me. I thought, "If he thinks this is good, wait until he sees the lights." I reached in my pocket and plugged in my skirt. Everybody stopped dancing and looked at us! He was mortified. The rest of the evening is a blur, and finally his parents took us home. I don't recall that my date ever spoke to me again. I can see his point, but I still think it was a great outfit. Somewhere in that thirteen-year-old, there's a little hint of perky dignity!

When you become dignified in a perky way, you cheer up. You shift your attitude to being positive. There's no reason to do this except your discipline. You just take delight in your world. You are being disciplined, and that's it. An executive said to me, "I always believe we're going to make the numbers until the last day. Then I only have one day of disappointment!" That's perky dignity. This style of engaging with the world increases your strength. And your confidence and optimism affect your world positively. Others around you cheer up, too. You're not denying reality—you're building up dignity! In Shambhala *the symbol for perky dignity* is a white snow lion with a huge turquoise mane to indicate your powerful head and shoulders and powerful upliftedness.

When an executive decided to change his company to respond to a market situation, he reflected for a long time and considered the risks carefully before he said, "Okay, I'm going to go out on a limb. Once I'm out there, I'll turn around and see who's following me." That's perky dignity. In another example, a man wanted to get married. He wasn't dating anyone, and so he asked another friend, "*How* am I going to get married? What should I *do*?" The second friend said, "Oh, that's easy. Enjoy yourself! Then look around and see who's standing right there with you!" That's perky, too. When a woman who is in her late nineties said to me, "I'm not afraid of dying, but I *am* curious," I thought, "That's perky dignity." A friend's mother was sick with Alzheimer's disease. When he went to see her toward the end of her life, she had something very important that she wanted to tell him before she died. She said, "When it gets too excited, try to relax. Then you get the joy of it." Then she added, softly, "I'm not sure I said that right." I think she did, indeed. That's perky dignity.

Outrageous Dignity

WHAT evolves next? More strength, more skill, more dignity. Your style of how to handle things begins to become *outrageous*.

Being cheered up and confident is now so much in your system that you're not watching yourself and measuring your progress anymore. No more thoughts of "Am I accomplishing any kind of bravery here? Could I cheer up more? How far have I come? Am I still clinging to anything? How far do I still have to go? Was I stronger yesterday? Are there others ahead of me?" Finally you stop trying to fabricate yourself in a certain way. You move beyond your ego's watchful eye. Now your style of engaging is outrageously dignified. You are willing to make mistakes, willing to step out of the norm, willing to go beyond whether you're being praised or being blamed. Your daring goes beyond ordinary logic. No one can interpret your logic anymore, and this includes you because you are not justifying what you are doing to yourself or anyone. Instead your practice is to relax and go beyond your limits, be brave and expand, extend without anxiety, cultivate tremendous relaxation. You are entering a timeless zone, which is an outrageous thing to do because you're surpassing conventional measurements.

There is a mythical bird in Indian culture called a garuda. A garuda is a strange-looking bird, very fierce, about the size of an owl, with big ears, big eyes and claws, wings fully displayed, and dark feathers. When the garuda is born, it bursts from its egg fully mature and flies and flies, without looking back. It doesn't look around to see how far it's come from the ground—it simply takes off and keeps flying. In Shambhala *the symbol for outrageous dignity* is the garuda. Like this bird that's born mature, you're no longer looking to see how far you've come. You're not competing with others, and you're not competing with yourself, so you celebrate freedom and humor in everything you do. Whether you act with or against convention isn't the point. You are no longer caught in hope and fear, so you're no longer caught anywhere.

The executive above who went out on a limb and changed his company was fired some years later. When he was fired, he refused to agree to a corporate release that said, "I'm leaving to spend more time with my family," so the company had to release the news without the usual storyline. Then he handmade a sign and hung it around his neck with a string, so the sign rested in front of his chest. The sign said, "Will work for food!" The final few weeks, instead of slinking away, he sat in the corner office with a great state of mind, just like always, and finished his work. One of the employees said later, "He was a prince in our corner!" His actions were more than perky—that's outrageous dignity.

Inscrutable Dignity

FINALLY *inscrutable dignity* unfolds. You have achieved enormous depth. Depth doesn't mean that you have become introspective. Whether you are "introverted" or "extroverted" doesn't even apply. Any pigeonhole that is offered is too small to describe what's happening with you. The usual pigeonholes of politics, economics, psychology, sociology, religion, leadership styles, personality types—all these concepts, *including* the concepts of basic goodness, *windhorse*, vision, and dignity, are too small to describe what's taking place within you. Now everything you do has become extremely unselfconscious and pragmatic. When action is needed, you perform it. When action isn't needed, you don't perform it. There is a profound sense of control, elegance, and dignity about you, purely because no more pettiness is left in your system or your view. No one can fathom your mind, including yourself, and you don't even try, because finally your mind isn't fixed on anything. It can't be characterized or captured. You've attained enormous relaxation and dignity.

Once I saw an old grandfather sitting in a garden playing with one of his grandchildren at the end of his life. The grandfather was like an old tree that's anchored in confidence, while the child was frisky, running around, and hadn't yet put down its roots. Inscrutable dignity is being like the grandfather or like an old deep-rooted tree on a hillside. You have settled into mastery. You accomplish your influence by generating a powerful atmosphere around you rather than running around, creating and promoting specific things. In Shambhala *the symbol for inscrutable dignity* is a dragon resting in the sky, playing with the elements. Dragons create weather and seasons. They create environment and influence things that way. The dragon moves, and it shifts the situation. When you have attained inscrutable dignity, you are solid and settled in your confidence. Your dignity is gentle, sympathetic, tender, and powerful. Sometimes Buddhist practitioners call this quality "being an old dog." The old dog barks when the situation needs it, and it doesn't bark when the situation doesn't need it. The environment around the old dog is either stirred up or settled down, whatever benefits.

When you attain inscrutable dignity, your commitment to the world is unwavering. At the same time, it is also noncommittal, because there's no big right or wrong in your view anymore—just lots of innuendo and play going on. This noncommittal quality is a quality of hollowness or emptiness. This hollowness is good. It's emptied out of overthinking and fixating on concepts, so you trust the emptiness. Now you can be completely pragmatic and playful with situations. At the same time, you have mastered yourself. You refrain from anything that unsettles your mind, so you are methodical and elegant. According to the Shambhala warrior texts, now your actions "bind situations like water, grow them like fire, refresh them like the wind, and sustain them like the earth." Your actions are like the actions of the elements. You realize that the space of your mind can never be grasped, so there's no longer any sense of separation from the world. You completely realize that the world is a friend. You relax tremendously, and the world's hospitality increases tremendously, too. Without having any stake in the outcome of actions, like a dragon in the sky—or like an old dog—you settle yourself confidently into the whole thing that's happening. You actually can experience that friendship and openness are everywhere. Trungpa Rinpoche said, for Shambhala warriorship and also Buddhism, "This is called enlightenment."

According to the Shambhala tradition inscrutable dignity is the pinnacle of what you can achieve as a human being. So much development has taken place that you rule your mind, you rule your speech, you rule your body, and now you rule your world—whatever comes up. Nothing, and no one, is regarded as separate from you, so nothing needs to be conquered or feared. Your entire activity at this point is to dispel whatever clouds confidence, promote whatever dignifies, and enjoy whatever benefits. That's it.

Meek, Perky, Outrageous, Inscrutable Dignity

ACHIEVING meek dignity is a tremendous relief. It's like landing on solid earth. Finally you are tender, strong, and humble. You feel good about yourself, so you don't need to be arrogant. Perky dignity is being very inquisitive to what's around you and very cheerful. You are not caught in doubting the infinite possibilities around you for inspiration and vision. Outrageous dignity is not hoping for a specific outcome. You've moved beyond hope, fear, and doubt, so you just launch yourself according to your vision. Finally, because of so much courage, daring, and thoroughgoing confidence you achieve the depth, solidity, and conquering of inscrutable dignity. You completely settle into being as you are. You completely accept the hospitality of the world. You are still an ordinary human being, but you might seem like a superhuman being to others because your humanity is so much in play. The effect on others is not that they are enamored of *you*. It's that when others are in your presence, they feel better about themselves! You achieve simplicity and compassion, and it has a powerful and beneficial effect.

I remember Rosa Parks. As the civil rights movement was beginning in the United States, one day she said, "No, not today. I'm very tired, and I'm not going to the back of the bus today." Day after day she went to the back of the bus, and then one day, "No, not today." At that moment in that bus on that day I think Rosa Parks had meek, perky, outrageous, inscrutable dignity. If she had taken her action without an inner journey, I don't think it would have had the same impact. Instead, her dignity that day was not simply Rosa Parks' dignity, or African-American dignity, or ex-slave dignity, or a woman's dignity, or a poor person's dignity, or a tired person's dignity. It was everyone's dignity— black dignity, white dignity, yellow dignity, brown dignity, red dignity, tired dignity, slave dignity, slave owner dignity, young dignity, old dignity, poor dignity, rich dignity. Every human being could stand a little taller because that day, without rage, without animosity, without shame, without a small self, she said, "No, not today. I'm not going to the back of the bus today."

No, not today. Sometimes Rinpoche called this meek, perky, outrageous, inscrutable dignity, "Couldn't care less." Usually, *couldn't care less* means just toss the Coke can out of the car window. Just one-up the other person. Just steal what you want. "Nothing matters. I won't get caught. Couldn't care less." But here *couldn't care less* means you're not trying to get something out of your action. You're not trading tit for tat. It's more generous than that. You act. You communicate. You take responsibility for the situation's well-being. You just do it. I once had a boss who said, "Don't worry if people like you or not. They won't like you anyway. Just do your job. Just try to move the company forward and be optimistic up until the day it doesn't work." Couldn't care less. Meek, perky, outrageous, inscrutable dignity takes out your hope and fear. You go beyond yourself, are inspired, and that's the dignity.

There is something in couldn't care less that is essential to being a courageous, powerful, and dignified human being. Sakyong Mipham Rinpoche, the current Shambhala lineage holder, said, "Couldn't care less is what allows you to get up in the morning and work for others' benefit without having a stake in the outcome. It allows you to transcend grasping. It allows you to take a fresh look. Without it you wouldn't be able to go beyond the dogma of basic goodness and really be of benefit." The artist Marcel Duchamp said that as an artist he created a work, but once the work was finished it was out of his hands. It no longer belonged to him, so he never listened to the critics. It's not that he felt superior. It's that now his work belonged to the public—couldn't care less. Couldn't care less is caring enormously. It is relaxing, expanding, and working with whatever comes up. Couldn't care less lets you step into fear. Couldn't care less provides the strength you need to shrug off your commentator and your cocoon. Couldn't care less allows you to open your senses and enjoy. Couldn't care less allows you to live and die with dignity. Couldn't care less means every moment is not separate from basic goodness. There is a totality of basic goodness in everything you do. Basic goodness depends on nothing. It just is what it is. Therefore your integrity, dignity, courage, and character are their own proof. Your genuineness is beyond logic—couldn't care less.

With meek, perky, outrageous, inscrutable dignity you are not trying to win over the other person or conquer the world. Everything is more carefree and egoless than that. You work tirelessly with everything, yet you do what you do for its own sake, so reality takes place directly. Your action is powerful because you couldn't care less.

There is a phrase in show business—"Do your best, and forget about the rest." This expresses basic goodness and couldn't care less. "Do your best" is your activity in the moment, which always has purpose. And "Forget about the rest" is the wisdom that you don't live for a purpose. You live because you live. Because of the pervasiveness of basic goodness, you can actually relax and celebrate your life. An interviewer said to Fred Astaire, "It must be wonderful to be able to express yourself!" And he replied, "I don't dance to express myself. I dance because I dance." This is meek, perky, outrageous, inscrutable dignity and couldn't care less. When Mother Teresa said, "God doesn't want you to succeed, he only wants you to try," she was expressing immense purpose and couldn't care less. When a lion roars in the jungle, all the other animals stop and listen. The lion isn't roaring to intimidate the other creatures. It roars because it roars, because that's what lions do. They are kings of the jungle, and they couldn't care less.

There is no authority for life. A vision of human goodness is intrinsic, but you can't come up with scientific evidence to prove it. Your unique vision is an expression of freedom and aspiration. Relaxing your *concept* of vision into the *practice* of your everyday life is attaining dignity and couldn't care less. The message of Buddhism and Shambhala is that you can relax into general, nonspecific goodness. This is how to create a dignified atmosphere around you and a decent common ground between you and your world.

The four warrior dignities introduced by Trungpa Rinpoche may sometimes seem out of reach, yet if we look a little closely, we can see the four dignities in our makeup. Like everything we have talked of, a wealth of human goodness and human power is already in us. You only need to bring it out. Whenever you have friendliness to yourself, then friendliness to your world happens simultaneously. A natural goodness begins to dawn in your heart, and a sense of dignity begins to occur. The more you open yourself up to this process, the more you find that the world extends its hospitality for you to proclaim your dignity. "No, not today. I'm too tired. I'm not going to the back of the bus today." Finally the power in human dignity is not a burden or unnatural. It is enjoyable. It is how to be a fully awakened human being.

17

A Lineage of Bravery

·■· ·■· ·■·

Ground: Hearing teachings on our humanity,

Path: Testing what we hear, and taking what's
meaningful to heart,

Fruition: We realize that a lineage of bravery
has always been there to help.

NO one is maturing solo. No one is a turquoise flower blossoming exquisitely in the air without the help of dirt, water, sunshine, and roots that came from seeds that were cared for and
produced an effect. We blossom because others help us. This is
also experiencing the world as friend.

In Shambhala, Buddhism, and other humanist traditions, simply by being decent you absorb the transmission of wisdom from
the world around you as you gain growing confidence and dignity.
Also, the transmission of wisdom is a traditional and deliberate

process where human beings pass their understanding to you in a direct and simple way. They share their realization, which is based on their own trials and tribulations and what was handed down, person-to-person, to them by someone else. It is a gift. Yet when you receive it, it's not that something foreign is being given to you. You don't say, "Gee, this is completely foreign to me! I didn't have this until you came along, and now I do." Instead, it awakens a power that's already in you. Your role in receiving the gift is to acknowledge what you already have. It's as if you were being reminded of something that you forgot, and you say, "Oh, you're talking to *me*. That's *my* heart you're talking about." You feel that you can realize the same thing if you stretch or shift a little bit.

The traditional analogy is as if you were a human being growing up among apes, and another human being came through the forest and told you, "You could be going upright. You could be cooking with pots and pans and wearing clothes like me. You could speak the human language, too." At first you'd be uncertain. Then you'd try it, and you'd find out that it's natural and it works. You are not receiving confirmation as if you completely possessed what you've been told. It's more like awakening something in you that transcends your present circumstances.

This is the experience of belonging to a *lineage*. Lineage means belonging to a family, inheriting what is yours, continuing something that has gone before. It is an ongoing situation. It is a process of being helped, learning, maturing, working with your potential, and inspiring yourself. Something awakens your potential, which you then have to bring into being, so in this sense you are the creative force. Still, you are empowering yourself based on the guidance, example, and generosity of a long line of other human beings.

Traditionally there are three ways of experiencing a lineage and receiving or hearing teachings. When you first hear the teachings, you're like the child who grew up in the forest with apes. Up to now your life has been whatever it has been. You have your friends and your patterns, and you do what you do. Then someone comes through the forest and talks directly and bluntly to you. It awakens your curiosity, and you try to understand. "Uh, uh, uh," but you don't get it. You feel puzzled and uncertain. "What are you saying? Why are you bothering to talk to *me*?" This is one way to experience lineage and hear its teachings.

The second way is that you take the teachings in, and somehow you get the whole thing upside down. You don't get it right. It's as if you were told, "You could be a fully human being like me," and instead you think, "You mean I can beat on pots and pans, and put those khaki shorts on my head?" When the lineage figures say, "Be yourself," you hear, "Change who you are." When they say, "Slow down your impulses," you hear, "Go with the energy in you. Act it out." When the lineage says, "A gentle light touch," you tell yourself, "Toughen up, and do it right."

The third and final way is when inspiring and empowering yourself finally begin to take root irreversibly. You hear something that sparks a fresh and precise experience in you. There is a gap where something sinks in. Finally, you understand that it's up to you to change. The result is that you begin to partially understand what's being given to you. Now your curiosity changes into longing because you long to realize yourself in a certain way.

There's no fourth way to experience a lineage and hear its teachings. This makes total sense! If you fully understood, you'd *be* the teachings. They wouldn't be separate from you anymore. If you realized something one hundred percent, the teachings would disappear. The wisdom would no longer be outside you. This is called *realization,* when you and wisdom are the same. Until then, you go with what you *do* understand, and the rest gradually comes along. You ponder, examine, test, make mistakes, learn, practice, take things personally, are objective, are subjective, mix teachings with your familiar world, and are brave and extend as you relax into a lineage's hospitality and engage more with your world. That way you make what has awakened in you immediate and real. You bring together what you've been told and what you've experienced. You take the teachings personally in order to find their meaning. "What does this mean to me? Is what I'm hearing true? Can it help me? Can I use it today? Does it apply in the situations I have? Can I use this in my home, in my work, with my peers, with my kids?" As you do this, you develop a sense of truth and strength. This is an instantaneous experience, like having spontaneous insight. It is also a gradual process that unfolds throughout your life. In belonging to a lineage you are trying to bring these two together—understanding directly what's being presented, and also testing what's been told within the context of your own experience, being objective and also trying out things personally, in order to gain confidence and stability in what you realize.

This process is like learning about the four dignities of Shambhala, or the four noble truths of the Buddhist tradition, or learning anything that's meaningful. You take it in, digest it, and make it part of you. You wear out the concepts like you wear out an old shoe, until finally you know what something *means,* both in your life and in the lineage it came from. Now if someone asks you, you can say what's been told, what's been experienced, and what it means to you. "My grandfather told me this, and his father told him. It's come to make a lot of sense to me."

You can never fully capture the depth of what's been handed to you, just as you can never fully capture the depth of yourself, and so this journey never ends. You realize a lineage of bravery has always been there for you, helping and providing guidance and direction by example, for a very long time. If you remember to keep a sense of this with you, in the atmosphere, constantly, all the time, you can develop a sense that this world actually is a friend. You will realize a sense of richness and purpose to your life.

When we try to count the people who have helped us, it doesn't really work. Recently I tried to count my obvious teachers: Chögyam Trungpa Rinpoche, Shunryu Suzuki Roshi, Dilgo Khyentse Rinpoche, Sakyong Mipham Rinpoche, Khandro Rinpoche, Kanjuro Shibata XX Sensei, Don Americo Yabar. But the project slipped out of my hands. My mother, who is a teacher to me, my father and family, Jakusho Kwong Roshi, Reverend Sing Hung, friends who teach me a lot, people I don't get along with who teach me, Milarepa, who lived a long time ago, the Buddha, who lived longer ago still. It's endless. I thought my first North Star was Trungpa Rinpoche, and now I see there are galaxies and galaxies there to guide us. A lineage of human bravery has always been there to help.

A friend told me that when the United States' Declaration of Independence was signed, the Iroquois Indians told Benjamin Franklin there were four rights to be cherished—the right to be, the right to grow, the right to learn, and the right to one's own wisdom. The Iroquois were handing on a vision to work with the totality of the world in an enlightened way. In 1993 I heard an interview on National Public Radio with a recent immigrant from Latin America. He said, "My dream is to have my family live in a peaceful situation, educate my children, contribute to my community and larger society, and help reduce the destructive forces in the world." I thought he expressed the same vision as the Iroquois Indians beautifully—a vision of a lineage of human bravery.

Each of us has been helped and guided for a long time, or we wouldn't have made it this far. Realizing this requires personal involvement and a slow, humble, and dignified journey. Finally, the journey produces tremendous gratitude. It makes our humbleness and longing increase immensely. This is different than longing for a new purse or a pleasant holiday. It's different than romantically longing for yourself in a certain way. At first it feels a little sheepish, that you have missed the point for so long—your longing is love and gratitude. A lineage of bravery has cared for you, encouraged you, wiped away your tears, taught you, and tried endlessly, with humor and compassion, to help you understand. The relationship with you is human, and their help is an act of love.

PART FIVE

It's Our Turn to Help

·■·

18

Change and Transformation

·■· ·■· ·■·

Ground: As we look at the notions of purpose and change,

Path: We see that changing ourselves is key.

Fruition: When change is personal and transforming,
it has a greater and beneficial effect.

IN order to mold and shape your world according to a greater
purpose and greater vision than usual, you have to do it from the
inside out. If you come at changing things as someone who has
superior knowledge, your arrogance only makes things worse.
You get feedback from the world and from within yourself to
find a better way. The same is true in the natural world. When
the sun invites plants to open up and blossom, the sun gives its
energy as an open gift. When the sun wields its force, using its
superior power and stature, the plants wither. The path of

greater vision has to be rugged and individual. First, *you* have to change the environment *you* project. As a warrior, you have to stay in nowness and make your gesture from there.

Nowness is not a way of seeing the truth, as if the truth were outside you. Nowness is *being* true. Genuine change, leadership, and vision are true for *this* nowness, *this* challenge, *this* moment. The magical thing about nowness is that when you opened up, the level of reality with which you're in contact changes. You change, and the level of reality with which you are working changes, too. It's like the caterpillar that transforms itself enough to go through an opening in the cocoon. When inside a cocoon, longing for fresh air, the caterpillar has an inkling of what might be ahead but doesn't really know that the sun is always shining and the sky is always vast. Once it goes through the opening, it finds itself in a larger world and it can fly and fly. Like the caterpillar, before you discover your courage, you think that your reality is small and dim. Instead, the sun's rays are always everywhere. The sun is shining all the time—just *you* were in the dark. Nothing has changed, except *you* perceive differently. *You* open up.

Sometimes we think of change mechanically or mathematically: one state or entity is replaced by another. "A appears. B appears. B replaces A. A disappears. What can a person do?" It's as if you say, "I used to be like that. Now I'm like this. I don't know how it happened. It's completely mysterious to me!" In fact, the mechanical model *is* mysterious. Where did A go? Where did B come from? This model of change is based on output rather than process. You add up all the outputs from specific points in time: "result A" + "result B" + "result C." If the total results aren't good, "Hmmm, too bad for me." If the total results are good, "I get a star!" Instead of change as an organic process of transformation, productivity is the VIP.

In many situations this model of change is useful, but our experience of change is different than this. Ice doesn't just disappear and water suddenly appear. Health doesn't just disappear and sickness suddenly appear. Our experience isn't mechanical like this. Experientially, our process of change doesn't really begin at some specific point, and it never really ends. It unfolds and unfolds, and along the way we make personal discoveries. Each time we make a personal discovery, we change. And each time we change, the reality we're in touch with changes, too. It's a mutual world.

I'd like to introduce briefly three ways of looking at change. One way is change where the situation has clear rules. For example, you are building a fence in your yard, giving a presentation at your church or work, washing your car, cooking a meal, fixing a faulty rocket, or pouring a cup of tea. It doesn't really matter. The situation you have is coherent. It has clear boundaries and a clear purpose. The rules are pretty much known, the time frame is somewhat short, and the process you are using is pretty well laid out. You feel you can operate in a manual, step-by-step way because the causality in front of you is clear. "If I do A, B will happen, because that's what has happened in the past." "If I don't check tomorrow's weather first, it doesn't make sense to start on the fence. It may snow or become too hot." "If we don't check the weather first, it doesn't make sense to launch the rocket, because the O-rings may fail." "If I cook this meal, I'll need to buy groceries first." "If I invite him to dinner, I'd better not serve shellfish because he's allergic." As far as action is concerned, you feel you can make a plan, and if you follow the plan, you'll get the results you predict.

This is *closed-ended change*. The cycle of learning is clear. You can run the process, look at the results it gives you, and learn what you need to learn for the next time. If it's too hot to paint the fence, next time start earlier in the day. If you need oriental sauce and you don't have it, just change the recipe. If you want your boss to think about causal relationships, make the message from the data jump off the page. Each time you complete the process—build a fence, cook a meal, launch a rocket—you have an opportunity to learn. The more often you run the process, the more you increase your knowledge of the process in different conditions and the more opportunity you have to learn about how to get your desired results. In closed-ended change, you are a spectator of change. You look at the results, learn, and over time you become more proficient at what you do. Depending on the situation and your vision, this is definitely a way of helping this world.

Another way of looking at change is like standing on a beach, looking at the open horizon. This situation is more open-ended. You are still a spectator of change, only now you're not so focused on results alone. The task is to be open moment to moment in order to learn what you need to know to accomplish what you intend. Examples are figuring out a murder mystery, exploring a trend in the market, trying to understand a trend in your teenager's behavior, planning the attendee list for a negotiation, or brainstorming a new product, process, or system at work. Because you are investigating, inventing, innovating, or trying to understand something new or unknown, the causality is less certain. "If I do A, I'm not sure what B will be." The opportunity to learn is more pervasive, and the consequences of your actions are less predictable. This is a more creative situation because the rules of change are more questionable. This is *open-ended change,* and there are different ways to deal with it. In addition to the desired results, your objective is to be flexible, strengthen your learning capacity, and be able to improvise what's needed. Depending on the situation and your vision, this is also a powerful way of helping this world.

A third way of looking at change is more personal. Now you are in the middle of the change, and it's more penetrating to the heart. Your point of view is still objective, like being a spectator of change in the examples above, but it's also subjective because you realize you're at the center of what's happening around you. You have change happening at the level of events, change happening at the level of patterns of events, change happening at the level of the whole system, and now there is change happening at the level of *you*. "Holy Cow, I'm in the *middle* of this. What's *happening*? And what should I *do*?" This change is more like you have parachuted out of a space ship. Here change isn't an option because it's happening already. You are floating in space, and you can't cultivate or prevent anything. The change is happening to you, but so what? Who cares? It's choiceless. There's nowhere to go, no one to praise, and no one to blame. Things are what they are, like it or not. Whether your parachute opens or not is not the point. Even when it opens, you're still floating in space. Like it or not, you are alone with it. Now your *heart* has to work hard and not purely your brain. This kind of change is personal and transforming. Depending on your point of view, the situation is either cause for celebration or a bad joke.

This third kind of change is *profoundly open-ended change*. It is a very penetrating experience. Now the change is at the level of raw reality, where the environment isn't separate from you and you don't control anything, not in the mechanical sense anyway. This is now change you are *in*. The causality is irrelevant because so what? What's happening is happening beyond cause and effect. No matter what you do, all you get out of the situation is yourself. In profoundly open-ended change your only choice is to be real, open, confident, courageous—all the things we've talked about—and to stay in touch with real reality. So you become completely pragmatic. Finally you are free, and equally you are trapped. Your mind is awake. Your heart is open. You can project your warmth and clarity fearlessly because you have nothing to gain or lose, so you can be brave, be relaxed, and expand. And that's it.

When you come into nowness, you don't know what the outcome will be. Your learning is heightened because now your actions are more in the context of reality. I had a boss who said, "Be confident, optimistic, and superior. That's what will help people." But how do we do this? On what basis? Gimmicks don't last, and waiting for wisdom doesn't work. Ultimately all you can do is extend as you are. How open you are depends on how much openness you can handle. The advice really is, "Be *genuinely* confident, optimistic, and superior *now, as you are*—that's what will help people." Just make yourself at home in profoundly open-ended change. It will pare you down to genuineness, and then you'll be able to help.

Several years ago, when I was trying to handle some difficulties in personal relationships and relationships at work, a friend took me to see a Chinese Buddhist abbot. He gave me this advice: "You have to hold your seat when circumstances of obstacle arise. If you hold your seat, obstacles can bring accomplishment—and this accomplishment brings more obstacles. So you might be carrying 120 kilo, while someone else has 100 kilo. Out of this, accomplishment may arise but watch out! Soon you may have 140 kilo!" He talked about becoming self-sufficient, like the Buddha, and how because the Buddha achieved self-sufficiency, therefore we could do this, too. He told me to hold my seat when the winds of circumstances blew; then everything would be serene. "Then you can affect the circumstances around you and bring things along."

This abbot had been an obscure monk whose teacher sent him to Canada for reasons I didn't know. He began living in a small hut on the outskirts of Toronto. Gradually the city of Toronto grew up around him. My friend's mother, who was a very devout Buddhist, moved to Toronto from South America, their family business flourished, and one evening she gave a party. A guest noticed her Buddhist shrine and said, "There's a monk living in the woods nearby who is a very devout meditator. You should visit him." She visited him, and each time she visited, she asked, "Can I help you?" Each time he declined. One day she said, "This hut isn't even heated for the winters. I have very powerful friends. Isn't there *something* I can do?" This time he said, "There *is* one thing." And he described his vision of a traditional Chinese Buddhist temple in Toronto, with one difference—the temple would have rooms where lay people could do weekend meditation retreats. She raised the money, today the temple is very powerful, and people do meditation retreats. An important Tibetan Buddhist teacher later visited Toronto from India. His hosts decided to take him to this Chinese Buddhist temple, not knowing the story of its background. When the Tibetan party walked into the temple, the Tibetan teacher bowed his entire body to the floor. This was unexpected from such an important person, so his attendants hurried to bow down, too. Three bows are traditional for Tibetans, so the attendants bowed three times. But when the attendants stopping bowing, the Tibetan teacher kept going.

When I think about this abbot's life, who and what were being transformed? A whole complex of situations was transformed— the obscure monk who became an abbot, the lady devotee, Toronto, the Chinese Buddhist community, and a visitor like me. The obscure monk took his seat in profoundly open-ended change; it had an effect; and the whole situation transformed. The inner journey of a single individual can have a tremendous outer effect. Had he not taken change to heart, that it was *he* who had to change, nothing would have happened. Instead he said,

"I'm in the middle of this. It's up to me. What can I do to help?" And everything around him transformed.

Trungpa Rinpoche taught that it's important to concentrate on the innate vision that we share with other human beings. One time he added, "Which makes up about twenty percent." This twenty percent isn't something you can separate out, refine, and fix to make it grow, like in the model of closed-ended change. Your twenty percent pervades you, and my twenty percent pervades me. It's all mixed in. Your lack of confidence isn't one thing, while your confidence is something else. It is the sense of lack itself that transforms into confidence. The person you are at the beginning of your journey isn't the one at the end. Your confusion becomes wisdom. Your fear becomes fearlessness. The alchemy is personal. Making an actual journey is like going to school or growing up. First you go to grade school. Then, on the basis of what you learned there, you advance to middle school, high school, and so on. First you learn to balance on your bike. Then you learn to race the other kids. You're not replacing one learning with another, or leaving it behind. You are growing your understanding, growing your realization, changing yourself. It takes a lot of skill to do this for oneself, and it takes even more skill to do this for another human being. To help others, I think we largely have to come at it by changing the environment they experience and affect things that way. Just having personal courage yourself provides a model for others. Just *you* projecting a ground of kindness provides ground for others to open up, too.

At Tassajara, the mountain retreat center started by Suzuki Roshi, there was a cook who was a very good Zen practitioner and very fierce. While living in a meditation center, the taste and value of food become very important, so if the food isn't satisfying, people steal into the kitchen at night to see what they can get. I heard a story about how this cook used to sit on top of the refrigerator during the night with a baseball bat, waiting to catch hungry practitioners. One day the cook said to Suzuki Roshi, "Roshi, the kitchen's a mess!" And Roshi said, "If you want to clean up the kitchen, first you have to clean up your mind." Serpico, the famous New York City policeman who blew the whistle on police department corruption years ago and later was the subject of a major Hollywood movie, was interviewed on the radio. The interviewer asked Serpico what it felt like to change the New York City Police Department. He said, "I didn't change the police department. I changed myself!" My refrigerator art used to include a newspaper photo of an African-American lady from Detroit, a city with a long history of prejudice, conflict, and extremes of wealth and poverty, power and powerlessness. She wore a sweatshirt that said, "The health of my community is up to me." These are examples of profoundly open-ended change, change that's personal and transforms you, so now your greater vision can have an effect on others, too.

You don't have to try to win over the other person, conquer the world, or dominate the team. Do what you do for its own sake. That way you can be powerful, be open to the situation, and help. As you engage directly with the world you will always be living in the challenge of change and transformation. Even if you live alone, it's a warrior's world. There's no place to take a break.

19

The Genuine Leader

·❖· ·❖· ·❖·

Ground: By bringing out the genuine leader
in ourselves and others,
Path: We accomplish our activity as an open gift.
Fruition: Compassionate activity arises—we are able to help.

WHEN you accept all situations into your heart, this doesn't mean you have a poor sense of boundaries. It means you are open-minded and openhearted, and therefore you are able to accept and work with what happens with wisdom and skill. In Shambhala this is sometimes called achieving *a monarch's view,* where the state of mind you have attained is both exalted and very simple. You are able to look down and see the whole world in a completely real way. When things get complicated, *you* are the one who simplifies, so you are like a monarch with a broken heart because you give up your fixed beliefs. You still are guided by greater purpose and greater vision, yet there is nothing specific to attain or maintain, so a deep longing, openheartedness, and willingness to work with others happen naturally. And because you have given up ego and fixed beliefs, you achieve something in return—command of your world. You become genuinely able to take the lead and help this world.

In the Shambhala teachings no one of us can just jump into leading others with wisdom and skill. There is a whole process you have to go through of learning how to handle yourself in real situations, gaining experience, making mistakes, gaining wisdom, establishing a seat from which to communicate, demonstrating fairness, gaining credibility, becoming trustworthy, developing authority, being able to provide a perspective for others, and so on. A lot of things have to happen and then, finally, there you are.

When we look around, we can see different kinds of leaders in the world. One kind has power over others and rules by intimidating them. Trungpa Rinpoche called this *P.O.O., power over others.* This leader is a bully who enslaves others. Even if you or I don't say it publicly or to their face, this person is trying to rule negatively, with no regard for basic goodness. I knew an executive who said he used the mushroom theory of management. "Keep them in the dark and feed them s—t." Another one explained his leadership theory like this. "There are two kinds of companies—orgasmic ones, where the ride to the top is explosive, and country club ones, where the ride is slower and smoother, with a lot of benefits." These are both examples of negative leaders who rule by power over others, with no regard for life and the spiritedness of human beings who are working for them, and with no regard for how they affect their company.

A different kind of leader has power over others and yet rules benevolently. When the fireman shouts, "There's the exit—go!," this is benevolent rule. The fireman is saying, "I'm in charge. Don't resist me—move!," and he or she is trying to help you. When the parent says no to try to help the child, it means, "Cross this line, and there will be consequences." As the fireman or parent you are tuned in to a real energy that exists, and someone else is heading off limits, so your power comes first, not theirs. Rinpoche called this Basic No. As a leader you give your Basic No, and then you communicate, "Here's what's happening, and why. Here's what you need to learn." You are not afraid to use your power. You know that leaders and parents can't always communicate first and then use power, so you do it the other way—power first, and *then* communicate. You lead powerfully, with benevolence.

Finally, there is a kind of leader who functions to bring out the leader in another person. This is a result of your own inner process, courage, and dignity. You see possibilities in others because you have realized something about yourself. You try to help them realize that they are fully capable of being visionary and leading in their own way. This style is *genuine leadership* because it's soaked in a vision of the basic goodness of human beings. As a genuine leader you don't think the world is yours to manage and control. You aren't practicing leadership disciplines to build up your muscles for another time when you conquer the world. Your leadership qualities are purely inspired by what's happening *now*. You use the fireman's approach when it's appropriate, and you still are a genuine leader, because you are trying to plant seeds in the moment that have a benevolent effect. When you lead as the fireman or parent, your exercise of benevolent power is purely inspired by what's happening *now*, with *this* unique person, at *this* unique time and place, not by what you want to have happen some other time with someone else. You are trying to cultivate others as leaders. The key point to being a genuine leader is that you're not trying to fill the world with replicas of yourself.

Leading others is not easy. Once a friend asked Trungpa Rinpoche, "Now that I'm in the leadership position, how should I run this organization? What should I do? How will I know if I'm doing the right thing?" He said, "If your ego is hurting, you're on the right track."

The Shambhala analogy for genuine leadership is creating an environment where flowers open and grow toward the sun. The sun releases its warmth, and the flowers are encouraged to grow. Trungpa Rinpoche said, "It's as though the sun says to the plants, 'Everything is there for you, so you can cheer up and expand your vision. You can step out and learn, and learn, and learn. Please, be my guest. Feel free to manifest the beauty and richness that you are.'"

Once I was asked to give a public talk on enlightened society. On a sudden inspiration I asked an executive at a company I was working with, "If you were giving a talk about creating an enlightened society, what would *you* say?" He looked at me a little strangely, then scribbled down the following.

1. Define terms to be used (i.e., society, enlightened, etc.).
2. Explain the value or benefits of an enlightened society on a broad (societal) and individual basis.
3. Be able to describe current society in a manner that is meaningful to the audience and then contrast it to an enlightened society.
4. Illustrate to the audience ways in which the individual can contribute to the change. Use examples that are specific.
5. Give permission to go slowly, to experience, to fail.

6. Quote teachings.
7. Leave lots of time for questions and discussion.
8. Suggest ways by which individuals can sense how they are doing as they strive to participate in the creation. Explore what the measures might be.
9. Urge people to be patient—this is a process subject to continual improvement!

As a genuine leader, he believed he had to lead by example and then invite and encourage others to do the same.

What you do in any situation depends on your unique situation, what the world presents to you, and how much bravery you have. Maybe you have enough bravery to lead your family unit, your company, or your country. That's good. Maybe all the bravery you have is just enough to meet a few surprises with kindness and curiosity as you take your dog on a walk. That's also good, not bad. Sometimes circumstances may bring you to your knees. You thought you were capable, and now all you can do is lie in your teepee and weep. All the other warriors are out being brave, and you can barely help the little insect that's landed in your soup. In all situations, finally, you are left with yourself. The entire Shambhala message is to feel encouraged about you and do what you can to bring out genuine leadership in others around you, too. Your action may seem insignificant, but you can't know its effect because everyone's journey, without exception, is personal. If you are being genuine, I'm sure it will help.

I met a man whose job was washing three hundred feet of sidewalk in downtown San Francisco once a week. He had been doing it for several years. Every day he washed it off, and about one hundred people walked by on the sidewalk. Sometimes he'd move his pail, and people would notice him and say, "What are you doing here? You're wasting water!" At the beginning, he took offense or had his feelings hurt. But he got to a point where he just was who he was with his pail on that street. He'd say, "Good morning," and each response from the passersby got to be totally okay with him.

One day he said to me, "There are some regulars—thirty or forty people I know who are just locked into an attitude that life is no damn good. I say good morning to those people, too. It may not change a thing, but I say it. It's like lighting a candle. If I light a candle, the light hits me. But the candle is not trying to shine on me. Whether I change or not is beside the point. It's just a candle, doing its thing. So I try to emulate that candle a little bit. It makes things lighter, not so heavy." Do what you can, like this sidewalk washer. Having a compassionate attitude is the way to celebrate human goodness, human virtue, leadership, and life.

In the Buddhist teachings compassion is often symbolized by the image of a full moon reflected in one hundred bowls of water. The moon isn't trying to benefit the bowls of water. It doesn't have a sense of audience, and it doesn't project a sense of demand. The moon isn't saying, "I'll shine on you if you give me something in return. Give me your attention. Give me your praise. Understand me. Love me." The moon is shining because that's its nature. The moon is just doing what it does, and the one hundred bowls of water are either murky or clear. When they are clear, they reflect the moon's light. When they are murky, they don't reflect the moon's light, but the light hits them anyway. It's an open gift. The moon does what it does freely, and it can activate the water in one hundred bowls to do the same.

Human virtue, leadership, and vision evolve in their own way, with their own logic. In the analogy of the full moon and bowls of water, they are multiplied, or not, one hundred times. The moon isn't in charge of what happens in the bowls, and yet the moon masters the situation. The one hundred bowls could be one thousand or one million bowls. The moon's light is compassionate, spontaneous, and endless in that way. The water in the bowls may say to the moon, "Yeah, yeah, but what about *me*? Tell me what to *do*!" However much the water pleads, the moon says, "I am sharing freely what *I* do. What *you* do is completely up to you."

When your activity of leadership is genuine, it's like the full moon. The effect of your activity falls where it falls. Rosa Parks did what she did that day, like the moon, and others took heart because of her. In genuine leadership your inner discipline has an effect, and others awaken or not, in their own activity, for their own purpose, in their own way. Compassion has no hierarchy or one-upmanship of "I am a leader, you are a nonleader" or "Lucky me, poor you." It doesn't have a goal in mind. Compassion is warmth that is released without a reason. It's part of you relaxing your being tremendously, and just doing your thing. It is generous in this way. Without exception the genuine leader is generous. It takes generosity to work with your relatives, your friends, your enemies, your kids, your boss, your spouse, fellow employees, the person you pay your bills to, and the lady up the block.

In the Buddhist tradition there are three kinds of generosity. These are related to leadership because they are ways to help another human being. Each is a kind of wisdom you can practice. Each one is free of ego or free of a lot of stuff about how "I'm great, because I am giving something to someone else." You don't need to lay a trip on yourself or anyone about being generous. Just open up and expand.

The first type of generosity is to give others what they need— a smile, a drink of water, a helping hand, freedom from hassling, honesty, forthrightness, hope. Whatever it is, this not something you have to reason out. "Hmm, let me think about this. Maybe they really need to hear about Marxism." "They want a glass of water from me, but hmmm, maybe they really need to pull up their own socks like good capitalists." "They need human kindness, but the more I think about it, they really need to join my crusade." Don't think about it! Just be generous, based on the humanity you share. Give them what they need.

The second type of generosity is to give fearlessness or to remove fear. Immediately after the World Trade Center in New York City was destroyed, Mayor Rudolph Guiliani told New Yorkers, "Go about your life. Go out. Don't be bound inside. We are going to open as much of the city as possible. We need to understand what's happened. Don't turn on your neighbors. We are a city of diversity. Don't be afraid." People felt a sense of security and stability from his presence.

The third type of generosity is to help others realize truth or reality without losing heart. This isn't just about external things. It's at a subtle level, too, which is harder to see. When you help others connect with their situation as it is, how they might need to grow, and the wisdom they themselves already have to deal with it, you are being generous. You are giving what others need, taking away their fear, and giving truth.

No one of us can just jump into leadership, do good, and create benefit. That's very rare. Instead you have to work to create the causes, conditions, and circumstances through which benefit can occur. This begins with peace and harmony in yourself, so you are able to see things as they are. Then you can lift your vision, look around, and have the courage to help.

You don't have to head into deep waters to be a genuine leader and benefit others. But you do have to incorporate life's subtleties. You do have to appreciate diversity. There is a wealth of richness, purpose, and leadership in other people, and you can help to bring it out. This kind of work is like opening a fan with multiple spines. Each spine is a point of strength that takes the lead, yet it is the whole fan that displays its beauty and the whole fan that moves the breeze. We are in this together, without exception, all of us.

20

It's Our Turn to Help

·◫· ·◫· ·◫·

Ground: A good society is possible.

Path: Being individually courageous, we help society to shift.

Fruition: In this way we can help this world—it's our turn to help.

THIS is a story about little frogs. In the story there are lots of little ponds and lots of little frogs in each little pond. All the little frogs in all the ponds know that there is depth, dignity, and truth to being, simply, a frog in a pond. A frog in one of the ponds knows. You are a frog in another one of the ponds, and you know, too. And you know that the frog next door knows, and you know that he knows that you know. On the other side of you, in the next pond, that frog knows, too. She knows that you know that he knows that you know that he knows, and you know that she knows, too. All the frogs in all the ponds know that you know that they know that you know! But nobody says it. Somehow the frog culture has gone out of sync with what the frogs simply are. This makes the frogs a little crazy, but it's not polite to say it. The way the frog culture has been going along seems smooth enough and all worked out. Some of the frogs proclaim they're in charge, and they say what the other frogs should be thinking. Along the way it has become too daring, too embarrassing, for the little frogs to proclaim frog dignity. What if the little frogs were wrong? Then one day, something modest but momentous happens in one of the ponds. One of the frogs proclaims frog dignity simply. Now it's possible for each little frog to be brave and dignified. It's been done before, and therefore each little frog can do it, too. Each little frog can be a genuine leader. The future of the frog society is completely open.

I think we're like the little frogs in the ponds. The spell of our culture and habitual patterns is very powerful. Yet a society based on depth, dignity, and truth isn't just an odd idea or a fantasy. People everywhere inherently want a good society and a good life. In the Shambhala tradition this vision is intrinsic in human beings—we only need to be courageous and bring it out, like the little frogs. The power of life is in the individual life that each of us has. You can be driving a taxi, doing the dishes, talking to your family, or addressing the press. The practice is for you to bring out your unique strength and courage in the situations you have and for me to bring out my unique strength and courage in the situations that are mine. There isn't anything else. Each of us actively creates society every day.

In the Buddhist tradition there are eighty-four people called *mahasiddhas* who lived in India many centuries ago. In Sanskrit *maha* means great, and *siddha* means an accomplished person, so these people were great practitioners with great realization. One of them was a prostitute, one was a weapons maker, one was a pimp, one was a king, one was a homeless person who slept for twelve years at a busy intersection in Delhi. Among the mahasiddhas in Tibet, Milarepa was a murderer who had remorse, Marpa was a farmer with a bad temper, Yeshe Tsogyal was a princess who had insight, Gesar of Ling was a legendary warrior who had courage, and Gampopa was a doctor who became a monk. Each of their stories encourages me. You can be a Shambhalian and be a prostitute, a weapons maker, a pimp, a king, a homeless person, a murderer with remorse, a wealthy landowner, a princess, a general, a doctor, and a monk. No one is excluded, and nothing you experience is excluded. Each of us can work with whatever situation we have. It's *how* we do what we do that helps this world that needs our help.

Society is relationships or the energy between things. Buddhism calls this a *mandala,* which is Sanskrit for collective experiences that are put together in an enlightened or unenlightened way. Shambhala simply calls this a society. The basic notion is that everything in your world is interdependent and interconnected with everything else. Nothing is excluded—trees, wildfires, pipelines, waterways, animals' activities, humans' activities, the sun, sky, gas stations, trucks, forests, weather, spiders, fizzy drinks, and the energy between all these is society. There are multiple societies inside your body. Society includes how countless cells, bacteria, and world systems exist in relationship. Society even includes the microscopic life inside your living-room couch, on a leaf on the tree outside your window, and in a section of dirt in your garden. Society is that whole complex of relationships and energies between the animate and inanimate, tangible and intangible, seen and unseen. The energy between everything is society. From this point of view, society is natural and fundamental. It doesn't refer to human society alone.

Shambhala, however, has a human focus. The driving creative force of Shambhala is to create a decent or enlightened *human* society on this earth, where the relationships between yourself and your environment are based on basic goodness and a vision that promotes the goodness of life. *Enlightened* means that a brilliant or awake quality is able to come through. The social vision of Shambhala is to organize all relationships on the basis of all-pervasive basic goodness, so the lines of communication are always open. The biggest obstacle to a good society is therefore aggression. Aggression is not the same as anger, which is part of the energy of life. Anger is part of your good workable human equipment. But aggression is different. The purpose of aggression is to cut off communication and destroy relationships. Whether the aggression is toward your environment, toward others, or toward yourself, its function is to kill the energy of society, so you have to take aggression out before a decent society can flourish. This responsibility begins with ourselves.

Usually we think someone else is in the lead, someone else is in charge. "That person has the power to influence others. I am nobody!" But you are in the lead in your own world. A single moment of genuineness on your part can have an enormous impact. Something splendid and dignified in your activity goes, "Psst, psst, psst" to your neighbors, and someone in the neighborhood goes, "Did you see that?" and the world goes, "Psst, psst, psst," and passes it along. Like a frog in one of the ponds, you influence things that way. You may not know the effect you have, and it may not be what you think. But what you do, and how you do it, is contagious; it has an effect. Therefore, the most important thing you can do is to have a view of basic goodness and communicate that in every thought and action that you do.

This world we have is a good world, and it is also in terrible shape. There are wars, famines, murder, new diseases, massive flows of armaments, children who aren't cared for, corruption, and endless individual grief. It's a mess. Still, it isn't a hopeless situation. Basic goodness is in you, in others, and in the environment. It pervades everything. Basic goodness doesn't guarantee anything, but it does allow you to create either a good society or a degraded one. This is the basic teaching. You don't need to agree on how to hold your knife at the dinner table, what side of a conflict you want to win, or what thoughts to think. But you can agree that everyone without exception is basically good and workable. The approach is that each of us can afford to soften, give in to our humanity, and use it to help someone else.

I have a friend who is a psychotherapist in a large cosmopolitan city. She describes her day like this. "I have to say, there are not too many people out there who are happy. The only one I know is sixty years old, and he's mentally retarded. He does chores for people in the neighborhood, works at the grocery store, and gets a pension from his late father. He has some problems. He's schizophrenic so he hears voices, but he's happy. The others? They're married and dissatisfied. Unmarried and dissatisfied. Have children and are dissatisfied. Don't have children and are dissatisfied. Are poor and dissatisfied. Are rich and dissatisfied. They are not able to appreciate what they have. But what's weird is that he appreciates his life. He says, 'I'm happy spring is here and summer is coming.' Objectively he's the most pitiful person I see. People make fun of him on the street. They look at him and think, 'Yuck, I wouldn't want to be him.' But he really appreciates his life! They are young, good-looking, have a job, have a boyfriend or girlfriend, and they want medications because they're miserable. And I wake up feeling miserable, too. What's my goal? To give and not be drained!"

I saw a videotape of Mother Teresa's life. The film showed her going to an orphanage that was under fire in Lebanon after a ceasefire with Israel had broken down. It showed her in Calcutta caring for lepers. It showed her training novice nuns, saying that only women who are cheerful can be candidates for her order. Various Western photographers followed the film crew around. At one point a photographer was so moved, he suddenly broke ranks and said, "Mother, what can I do to *help*?" My mind went, "Money! She needs money for shelters!" But that's not what Mother Teresa said. She said, "Appreciate. Appreciate." Mother Teresa and my friend's client are teaching us the same thing. Everything is there to be appreciated, everything.

Creating a good society may seem like a big job, but society is relationships, so it begins very small. One little frog shifts, and the pond around it brightens up. There is no prescription, really, for waking up your world, except to be open and compassionate with your everyday challenges as much as you can. The shift happens in the everyday moment. You might be freeing an insect from your bathtub, standing in a checkout line at the store, choosing what tie to wear, cooking dinner, running a business, or organizing your neighborhood. You can try to experience basic goodness and the flowing of it in whatever you do. Every situation you are in, without exception, has this possibility. Khandro Rinpoche, a young Tibetan Buddhist teacher, said to a group of her students, "It's not that hard to be enlightened! Just change your patterns! All it takes is courage!"

As I reflect, I can see that other people are the same as I am, with the same kinds of problems and promise. Everyone is going through the same kinds of things. There are millions and billions of people who have the same kinds of conflicts and anxieties. In Shambhala an enlightened human society is not a paradise. It is not a realm of bliss where everything is lovely and no problems are experienced. A good society doesn't mean everyone speaks the same language, is knowledgeable about the world, and has a house with a green lawn, a lawnmower that works, a car in the garage, 2.5 children, a nice neighbor, and a chicken cooking in the pot. It's a web of diverse relationships that are reasonable and true and function to hold us together. A good human society is based on *this* world, the world we have, *this* one that is personal and real. It includes everything—conflict, poverty, wealth, the natural processes of birth, old age, sickness, and death, anger, passion, judges, and jails. What's different is that its potential is beyond what you or I can grasp—a healthy society, with problems that aren't seen as hopeless, where care and respect for each other and the environment are the foundation, and everyone is seen as being at some stage of developing individual bravery. This is not to say you don't relate with anything other than people's goodness, but your actions are based on the conviction that tenderness exists in everyone.

Enlightened society happens one by one, like the little frogs in the ponds. You shift. I shift. My neighbor shifts. Someone in Angola shifts. A person in Russia shifts, someone in the Philippines shifts. A gang member shifts. A Parliament member shifts. A mother shifts. A child shifts. A news commentator shifts. A prisoner shifts. A warden shifts. A homeless person shifts. Once you realize this, peacefulness and a deep respect for human beings are natural. The help that's needed is to help each person shift, and as they shift, they help the rest of us shift, too. There is no real recipe, except working with what the world presents from the point of view of basic goodness, compassion, and courage. The key is never to make a separation between your practice and your everyday life.

Finally, the world isn't a political world, an economic world, a first world, a third world, a domestic world, a work world, a natural world, an international world, a troubled world, or a beautiful world. It's *all* these and all other possibilities. This is more than the message of basic goodness. It is a message of vision. Creating a good society isn't easy, or everyone would be doing it. It takes an awake mind and open heart. It takes courage and dignity. As I have experienced this path, the practice is not about living a lukewarm life. "Yeah, yeah, the present, a vision, courage, dignity, ho hum." You are releasing the sun of basic goodness to shine freely in your life, and its effect is to warm the world. It may look like your everyday action has nothing to do with solving society's big problems, but it does. I said to a friend, "I wonder what I would do if I were caught in the Middle East war." He said, "There's no point wondering that. It's not real. You'd have to fabricate a situation, which is fabricating a thought. Then you'd have to fabricate a response. Then finally you'd end up with a fabricated position. That won't help." I thought, He's right. I have to do what I can do with what's in front of me. The relationship that can make a difference is personal.

One of my teachers, Sakyong Mipham Rinpoche, said it something like this: The world isn't biased. It just is what it is. We try to interpret it as good, bad, racist, not racist, rich, poor, masculine, feminine, fair, unfair, capitalist, socialist, for profit, not for profit, kind, cruel, boring, exciting—but fundamentally it just is what it is. The forms that teachings take will come and go. But the ongoing power of life is that the goodness, energy, and sacredness of life are always there for you. Finally, your individual softness and bravery *truly* are the way to be a fully human being. The more conviction you have in this, the more your courage and dignity have an effect in your everyday world.

The notions of awake mind and open heart are not new. They are largely common sense. They are part of the natural wisdom human beings have always had. Each of us can glimpse basic goodness, *windhorse* energy, and meek, perky, outrageous, and inscrutable dignity in our system when we are gentle, curious, and willing to look. It's as if there were a dynamic of enlightened energy underneath our everyday consciousness. The more we develop conviction in this, the more it helps. All that's required are appreciation and courage.

There is a story about a collection of paintings by Picasso that Picasso kept for himself. One of them is very small, only 7¼ by 5½ inches. It is a very dark oil painting with a figure of a man in the corner wearing a dark hat and overcoat. When asked about it, Picasso said that once the painting was big, "really big, monumental," and he gestured hugely with his arms. Then he said, "But that was long ago. I later painted it over with other subjects many times, then cut it into pieces and then painted it again. This is all that remains. It is my father." I find that the journey to live life in a meaningful way is like this story of Picasso's painting. One's vision deepens rather than diminishes over time, and the process of achieving our life's meaning isn't linear. I suspect this is true for all human beings. Each of us lives our awareness from continuously shifting points of view. Like Picasso's painting, you change your perspective on your life, change the colors, change the subject, cut it into pieces, and paint it again. Nothing is really final. From one point of view your life looks like a series of continuous mistakes! Yet the hard work of your heart to bring your life's meaning into focus makes the difference. Once you discover its heartfelt meaning, your life has stature. Then as you go about your everyday activity, the power and benefit of your actions increase immensely.

There are many practices you can do to support your journey. Sitting meditation will allow you to experience gaps, so you can see your soft spot. It produces clear seeing, so you can discern what is happening, what your humanity is, and how your world works. As your sympathy is ignited, this naturally extends into meditation in action. Then rousing *windhorse* will give you the energy you need to conduct your life with purpose and greater vision. Practice sitting meditation. Learn how to make friends with fear. Rouse *windhorse* once, twice, ten times, or one hundred times a day. Take change and transformation personally. Lead a genuinely inner-based inner journey. There are many, many ways to practice. Practice is like life. The more you do it, the more you learn. A friend asked a Zen practitioner with a very active life, "When do you practice?" She said, "I practice all the time."

The most important practice is continuity—realizing basic goodness, opening your heart and being brave. Once you realize that your basic nature has enlightened qualities, then you can work to create enlightened relationships. There is no real alternative to creating a good society. The world is waiting for you to discover greater vision in you, enjoy it, and put it to use. Shibata Sensei, my Japanese archery teacher, said about my archery bow, "Don't treat it like an object of veneration! Use it, use it, use it!" This is true for our purpose and vision, too. We have to use them. The world needs this at this time—it's our turn to help.

APPENDIX

HERE are the threefold logics for *Awake Mind, Open Heart*.

Ground. The first line of each stanza below represents a foundation or basic assumption in which the content of a chapter is grounded. For example, the second stanza, representing the first chapter, begins with, "The social vision of Shambhala has many meanings, and one of them is personal."

Path. The second line shows the path or method of attainment: "By finding its meaning in our experience."

Fruition. The third line describes a result or culmination: "We are able to uplift ourselves and our society."

■

INTRODUCTION

Ground: The teachings of Buddhism and Shambhala
are very profound.

Path: When we take them to heart,

Fruition: We can gain courage and dignity,
regardless of our circumstances.

THE MEANING OF SHAMBHALA

Ground: The social vision of Shambhala has many meanings,
and one of them is personal.

Path: By finding its meaning in our experience,

Fruition: We are able to uplift ourselves and our society.

BASIC GOODNESS

Ground: There is something unconditionally
good about ourselves.

Path: Experiencing our soft spot,
we glimpse a larger world.

Fruition: We can use these glimpses to discover
a path of courage.

BEING GENUINE AND TRUE

Ground: Being friendly to ourselves,

Path: We are genuine and true,

Fruition: And therefore we project harmony to our world.

A JOYFUL AND SAD HEART

Ground: Experiencing our experience fully,

Path: Our heart is joyful and sad.

Fruition: We develop conviction that a joyful-sad heart
is natural and good.

SETTLING DOWN WITH OURSELVES

Ground: All beings have the capacity to just be as they are.

Path: Meditating in this way,

Fruition: We increase our resourcefulness and strength.

AWAKE MIND

Ground: Mindfulness and awareness belong to human beings.

Path: By practicing peacefulness and insight,

Fruition: Intrinsic mindfulness-awareness unfolds as wisdom in our life.

HOW TO MEDITATE

Ground: Adopting an attitude of dignity,

Path: We train our body, speech, and mind in simplicity.

Fruition: This lays a good foundation for our humanity to unfold.

THE COMMENTATOR AND THE COCOON

Ground: Just seeing the commentator and cocoon

Path: Begins to weaken their strategy

Fruition: And produce sympathy toward ourselves and others.

PLANTING SEEDS OF FEARLESSNESS

Ground: Fear is seemingly ubiquitous in our life.

Path: Having the courage to get to know our fear

Fruition: We discover tenderness that is useful, realistic, and brave.

COURAGE IN EVERYDAY LIFE

Ground: Unconditional awareness is our nature.

Path: By unconditionally trusting our state of mind on the spot

Fruition: We become resourceful and brave in everyday life.

DISCOVERING GREATER VISION

Ground: Human beings are innately visionary.

Path: Cultivating openness, wakefulness,
and forward-looking discipline

Fruition: We develop a capacity to listen to and
communicate our wisdom.

MAGICAL *WINDHORSE*

Ground: Windhorse is inherent life-force or vitality.

Path: Increasing our connection to this universal energy,

Fruition: We are able to deal powerfully with
challenges and coincidence.

ATTAINING DIGNITY

Ground: Accomplishments generate charisma or presence.

Path: By making our inner journey without doubt.

Fruition: We radiate an atmosphere of
authenticity and dignity.

HOW TO INVOKE *WINDHORSE*

Ground: Windhorse generates a sense of life.

Path: By deliberately increasing its energy,

Fruition: We empower our purpose and our vision.

THE WORLD AS FRIEND

Ground: The world functions as a teacher.

Path: By opening further and extending ourselves.

Fruition: We discover our entire life is workable and a friend.

FOUR DIGNITIES

Ground: We use different styles of engaging our world.

Path: By being dignified in meek, perky, outrageous, and inscrutable ways,

Fruition: We can attain the pinnacle of being a fully human being.

A LINEAGE OF BRAVERY

Ground: Hearing teachings on our humanity,

Path: Testing what we hear, and taking what's meaningful to heart,

Fruition: We realize that a lineage of bravery has always been there to help.

CHANGE AND TRANSFORMATION

Ground: As we look at the notions of purpose and change,

Path: We see that changing ourselves is key.

Fruition: When change is personal and transforming, it has a greater and beneficial effect.

THE GENUINE LEADER

Ground: By bringing out the genuine leader in ourselves and others,

Path: We accomplish our activity as an open gift.

Fruition: Compassionate activity arises—we are able to help.

IT'S OUR TURN TO HELP

Ground: A good society is possible.

Path: Being individually courageous, we help society to shift.

Fruition: In this way we can help this world—it's our turn to help.

BIBLIOGRAPHY AND RESOURCES

Duncan, David Douglas. *Picasso's Picassos.* Lausanne: Harper & Brothers, 1961.

Kneen, Cynthia. *Shambhala Warrior Training.* Boulder: Sounds True Audio, 1996.

Suzuki, Shunryu. *Not Always So: Practicing the True Spirit of Zen.* New York: HarperCollins, 2002.

———. *Zen Mind, Beginner's Mind.* New York and Tokyo: John Weatherhill, 1970.

Trungpa, Chögyam. *Born in Tibet.* London: George Allen & Unwin, 1966.

———. *Cutting Through Spiritual Materialism.* Berkeley: Shambhala Publications, 1973.

———. *Great Eastern Sun: The Wisdom of Shambhala.* Boston and London: Shambhala Publications, 1999.

———. *Meditation in Action.* Berkeley: Shambhala Publications, 1969.

———. *Shambhala: The Sacred Path of the Warrior.* Boulder and London: Shambhala Publications, 1984.

Other Resources

cynthiakneen@yahoo.com, www.cynthiakneen.com

Naropa University, 2130 Arapahoe Avenue, Boulder, Colorado 80302, www.naropa.edu

San Francisco Zen Center, 300 Page Street, San Francisco, California 94102, www.sfzc.org

Shambhala International and Shambhala Training® International, 1084 Tower Road, Halifax, Nova Scotia, Canada B3H 2Y5, www.shambhala.org

Shambhala Mountain Center, 4921 County Road 68C, Red Feather Lakes, Colorado 80545, www.shambhalamountain.org

Shambhala Sun, 1585 Barrington Street, Suite 300, Halifax, Nova Scotia, Canada B3J128, www.shambhalasun.com

Sonoma Mountain Zen Center, 6367 Sonoma Mountain Road, Santa Rosa, California 95404, www.smzc.net

The Shambhala Institute for Authentic Leadership, 6029 Cunard Sreet, Suite 5, Halifax, Nova Scotia, Canada B3K 1E5, www.shambhalainstitute.org

ACKNOWLEDGMENTS

WRITING this book has been like having a long conversation to say a very simple thing. Along the way certain individuals have helped immensely. In particular I would like to thank Chögyam Trungpa Rinpoche, my root teacher, whose compassion changed the course of my life. These teachings belong to Chögyam Trungpa, and many of the phrases and metaphors I used belong to him. If I could repay one ounce of his kindness, I will have lived a decent life. I would also like to acknowledge the central role of Sakyong Mipham Rinpoche, the current Shambhala lineage holder, whose insight and poetic brilliance wake me up and to whom I feel extraordinarily grateful and loyal. In addition I would like to thank Shunryu Suzuki Roshi, who started me on this path; Kanjuro Shibata XX Sensei, whose fierceness is a little startling and who, like all my teachers, gave generously; the Venerable Khandro Rinpoche, whose compassionate friendship penetrates to the heart and who encouraged me; Jakusho Kwong Roshi, who extended an open hand in friendship when I asked; my publisher, Matthew Lore, without whose cheerful prodding, kindness, and quick insight this book would never have attained any honesty; David Schneider, the author of *Street Zen*, a dear friend whom I respect, love, and admire; my father, who gave generously to his children without asking anything in return; my mother, whose gentle and careful reasoning is a teacher to me; Christie Cashman, executive director of Shambhala Training, who provided early encouragement to the project; many of my friends, in particular Johanna Alper, Barbara Blouin, Jenny Bondurant, Gregg Eller, Eric Kotila, Adri Magnuson, Bernice Moore, Bob Morehouse, Oona O'Connell, and Alan Rabold; and finally, two talented women writers: Lola Wilcox, who made skillful and invaluable suggestions, and Ann Poe, a first-class pro at the writing process itself.

May the result be of benefit.